100 GREAT POEMS FOR BOYS

Also edited by Leslie Pockell

21 Essential American Short Stories
100 Essential American Poems
100 Poems to Lift Your Spirits
The 100 Best Poems of All Time
The 100 Best Love Poems of All Time
The 13 Best Horror Stories of All Time
Everything I've Learned
The 101 Greatest Business Principles of All Time
The 100 Greatest Sales Tips of All Time
The 100 Greatest Leadership Principles of All Time

100 GREAT POEMS FOR BOYS

LESLIE POCKELL

WITHDRAWN

GRAND CENTRAL
PUBLISHING

NEW YORK   BOSTON

Some poems have been reprinted by permission, which the editor and publisher gratefully acknowledge in detail in the Acknowledgments section of this book, beginning on page 229.

Grand Central Publishing
Hachette Book Group
237 Park Avenue
New York, NY 10017

www.HachetteBookGroup.com

Printed in the United States of America

First Edition: April 2011

10 9 8 7 6 5 4 3 2 1

Grand Central Publishing is a division of Hachette Book Group, Inc.
The Grand Central Publishing name and logo is a trademark of Hachette Book Group, Inc.

The publisher is not responsible for websites (or their content) that are not owned by the publisher.

Library of Congress Cataloging-in-Publication Data

100 great poems for boys / [edited] by Leslie Pockell.—1st ed.
    p. cm.
  Summary: "In the spirit of the Dangerous Book for Boys, here are 100 essential poems for boys of all ages"—Provided by publisher.
    ISBN 978-0-446-56382-6
  1. Boys—Poetry. 2. English poetry. 3. American poetry. 4. Children's poetry, English. 5. Children's poetry, American. I. Pockell, Leslie.
II. Title: One hundred great poems for boys.
  PR1195.B7A16 2011
  821'.00803521—dc22

2010036490

Contents

Fun to Read Aloud 45

Battlefields and Heroes 75

Things to Think About 133

Tongue Twisters 155

Limericks 163

Just for Laughs 171

Introduction

You don't have to be any special age to be a boy. It's more a state of mind than anything else (even certain girls can qualify, if they have the right attitude!). I was a boy quite a few years ago, and actually, it seems to me that in many ways I still am. I put together this collection largely by drawing on memories of the early days of my own reading experience. I remember the thrill of reading about the brave, doomed soldiers of the Light Brigade as they rode into glory, and wrestling with the seemingly inescapable logic that led to the ultimate destruction of the wonderful one-horse shay. I loved the witty and exotic tale of the Pied Piper of Hamelin, a dramatic and memorable mini-epic about the importance of keeping promises, and the action-filled story of the Roman hero Horatius defending the gates of Rome. Like most boys, I've also always loved nonsense poems—the silly ones, of course, like "The Walrus and the Carpenter" (though it has rather a dark moral), and especially the ones that are grounded in some kind of fundamental truth, like "The Blind Men and the Elephant." And learning rhymes, riddles, and tongue twisters are a wonderful part of growing up that we can hold on to as we get older. Reading any great poem for the first time is always a thrilling discovery, even if it's only four lines long, and this collection brings together some of the best ever written, memorized, or read aloud. I hope you enjoy reading these poems as much as I enjoyed putting them together in this book, whatever your age or gender, and that they will stay with you as inspiring or entertaining companions throughout your reading life!

ANIMALS

There must be some special reason why so many great poems are about animals. Maybe it's because even though animals look and act so differently from people, they still have many things in common with us—or at least we'd like to think so! They also are so different from one another: Animals are fierce, like Blake's "Tyger," or timid like Robert Burns's wee mousie. Eagles fly majestically and flies—just fly! But whether they're funny-looking like the platypus, mysterious like the raven, or a complicated puzzle of a beast like the elephant, animals have inspired some of the best poems ever written.

Epigram Engraved on the Collar of a *Dog* Which I Gave to His Royal Highness

Alexander Pope

I am his Highness' Dog at *Kew*;
Pray tell me Sir, whose Dog are you?

For My Cat Jeoffry

Christopher Smart

For I will consider my Cat Jeoffry.

For he is the servant of the Living God duly and daily serving him.

For at the first glance of the glory of God in the East he worships in his way.

For is this done by wreathing his body seven times round with elegant quickness.

For then he leaps up to catch the musk, which is the blessing of God upon his prayer.

For he rolls upon prank to work it in.

For having done duty and received blessing he begins to consider himself.

For this he performs in ten degrees.

For first he looks upon his fore-paws to see if they are clean.

For secondly he kicks up behind to clear away there.

For thirdly he works it upon stretch with the fore-paws extended.

For fourthly he sharpens his paws by wood.

For fifthly he washes himself.

For Sixthly he rolls upon wash.

For Seventhly he fleas himself, that he may not be interrupted upon the beat.

For Eighthly he rubs himself against a post.

For Ninthly he looks up for his instructions.

For Tenthly he goes in quest of food.

For having consider'd God and himself he will consider his
neighbor.

For if he meets another cat he will kiss her in kindness.

For when he takes his prey he plays with it to give it chance.

For one mouse in seven escapes by his dallying.

For when his day's work is done his business more properly
begins.

For he keeps the Lord's watch in the night against the
adversary.

For he counteracts the powers of darkness by his electrical
skin and glaring eyes.

For he counteracts the Devil, who is death, by brisking
about the life.

For in his morning orisons he loves the sun and the sun
loves him.

For he is of the tribe of Tiger.

For the Cherub Cat is a term of the Angel Tiger.

For he has the subtlety and hissing of a serpent, which in
goodness he suppresses.

For he will not do destruction, if he is well-fed, neither will
he spit without provocation.

For he purrs in thankfulness, when God tells him he's a
good Cat.

For he is an instrument for the children to learn
benevolence upon.

For every house is incompleat without him and a blessing is
lacking in the spirit.

For the Lord commanded Moses concerning the cats at the
departure of the Children of Israel from Egypt.

For every family had one cat at least in the bag.

For the English Cats are the best in Europe.

For he is the cleanest in the use of his fore-paws of any quadrupede.

For the dexterity of his defense is an instance of the love of God to him exceedingly.

For he is the quickest to his mark of any creature.

For he is tenacious of his point.

For he is a mixture of gravity and waggery.

For he knows that God is his Savior.

For there is nothing sweeter than his peace when at rest.

For there is nothing brisker than his life when in motion.

For he is of the Lord's poor and so indeed is he called by benevolence perpetually—Poor Jeoffry! poor Jeoffry! the rat has bit thy throat.

For I bless the name of the Lord Jesus that Jeoffry is better.

For the divine spirit comes about his body to sustain it in compleat cat.

For his tongue is exceeding pure so that it has in purity what it wants in musick.

For he is docile and can learn certain things.

For he can set up with gravity which is patience upon approbation.

For he can fetch and carry, which is patience in employment.

For he can jump over a stick which is patience upon proof positive.

For he can spraggle upon waggle at the word of command.

For he can jump from an eminence into his master's bosom.

For he can catch the cork and toss it again.

For he is hated by the hypocrite and miser.

For the former is affraid of detection.

For the latter refuses the charge.

For he camels his back to bear the first notion of business.

For he is good to think on, if a man would express himself neatly.

For he made a great figure in Egypt for his signal services.

For he killed the Ichneumon-rat very pernicious by land.

For his ears are so acute that they sting again.

For from this proceeds the passing quickness of his attention.

For by stroaking of him I have found out electricity.

For I perceived God's light about him both wax and fire.

For the Electrical fire is the spiritual substance, which God sends from heaven to sustain the bodies both of man and beast.

For God has blessed him in the variety of his movements.

For, though he cannot fly, he is an excellent clamberer.

For his motions upon the face of the earth are more than any other quadrupede.

For he can tread to all the measures upon the musick.

For he can swim for life.

For he can creep.

The Tyger

William Blake

Tyger Tyger, burning bright,
In the forests of the night:
What immortal hand or eye
Could frame thy fearful symmetry?

In what distant deeps or skies
Burnt the fire of thine eyes?
On what wings dare he aspire?
What the hand dare sieze the fire?

And what shoulder, & what art,
Could twist the sinews of thy heart?
And when thy heart began to beat,
What dread hand? & what dread feet?

What the hammer? what the chain,
In what furnace was thy brain?
What the anvil? what dread grasp
Dare its deadly terrors clasp!

When the stars threw down their spears
And waterd heaven with their tears:
Did he smile his work to see?
Did he who made the Lamb make thee?

Tyger Tyger burning bright,
In the forests of the night:
What immortal hand or eye
Dare frame thy fearful symmetry?

The Lamb

William Blake

Little Lamb, who made thee?
　Dost thou know who made thee?
Gave thee life & bid thee feed,
By the stream & o'er the mead;
Gave thee clothing of delight,
Softest clothing wooly bright;
Gave thee such a tender voice,
Making all the vales rejoice!
　Little Lamb who made thee?
　Dost thou know who made thee?

Little Lamb I'll tell thee,
　Little Lamb I'll tell thee!
He is calléd by thy name,
For he calls himself a Lamb:
He is meek & he is mild,
He became a little child:
I a child & thou a lamb,
We are calléd by his name.
　Little Lamb God bless thee.
　Little Lamb God bless thee.

To a Mouse

ON TURNING HER UP IN HER NEST
WITH THE PLOUGH, NOVEMBER 1785

Robert Burns

Wee, sleekit, cow'rin, tim'rous beastie,
O, what a panic's in thy breastie!
Thou need na start awa sae hasty,
   Wi' bickering brattle!
I wad be laith to rin an' chase thee,
   Wi' murd'ring pattle!

I'm truly sorry man's dominion
Has broken Nature's social union,
An' justifies that ill opinion
   Which makes thee startle
At me, thy poor earth-born companion,
   An' fellow-mortal!

I doubt na, whiles, but thou may thieve;
What then? poor beastie, thou maun live!
A daimen icker in a thrave
   'S a sma' request:
I'll get a blessin wi' the lave,
   And never miss't!

Thy wee bit housie, too, in ruin!
Its silly wa's the win's are strewin!
An' naething, now, to big a new ane,
O' foggage green!
An' bleak December's winds ensuin,
Baith snell an' keen!

Thou saw the fields laid bare and waste,
An' weary winter comin fast,
An' cozie here, beneath the blast,
Thou thought to dwell,
Till crash! the cruel coulter past
Out thro' thy cell.

That wee bit heap o' leaves an' stibble
Has cost thee mony a weary nibble!
Now thou's turned out, for a' thy trouble,
But house or hald,
To thole the winter's sleety dribble,
An' cranreuch cauld!

But, Mousie, thou art no thy lane,
In proving foresight may be vain:
The best laid schemes o' mice an' men
Gang aft a-gley.
An' lea'e us nought but grief an' pain
For promised joy.

Still thou art blest, compared wi' me!
The present only toucheth thee:
But och! I backward cast my e'e
          On prospects drear!
An' forward, tho' I canna see,
            I guess an' fear!

The Eagle

Alfred, Lord Tennyson

He clasps the crag with crooked hands;
Close to the sun in lonely lands,
Ringed with the azure world, he stands.

The wrinkled sea beneath him crawls;
He watches from his mountain walls,
And like a thunderbolt he falls.

The Blind Men and the Elephant

John Godfrey Saxe

It was six men of Indostan
　　To learning much inclined,
Who went to see the Elephant
　　(Though all of them were blind),
That each by observation
　　Might satisfy his mind.

The *First* approached the Elephant,
　　And happening to fall
Against his broad and sturdy side,
　　At once began to bawl:
"God bless me! but the Elephant
　　Is very like a wall!"

The *Second*, feeling of the tusk,
　　Cried, "Ho! what have we here
So very round and smooth and sharp?
　　To me 'tis mighty clear
This wonder of an Elephant
　　Is very like a spear!"

The *Third* approached the animal,
    And happening to take
The squirming trunk within his hands,
    Thus boldly up and spake:
"I see," quoth he, "the Elephant
    Is very like a snake!"

The *Fourth* reached out an eager hand,
    And felt about the knee.
"What most this wondrous beast is like
    Is mighty plain," quoth he;
"Tis clear enough the Elephant
    Is very like a tree!"

The *Fifth* who chanced to touch the ear,
    Said: "E'en the blindest man
Can tell what this resembles most;
    Deny the fact who can,
This marvel of an Elephant
    Is very like a fan!"

The *Sixth* no sooner had begun
    About the beast to grope,
Than, seizing on the swinging tail
    That fell within his scope,
"I see," quoth he, "the Elephant
    Is very like a rope!"

And so these men of Indostan
    Disputed loud and long,
Each in his own opinion
    Exceeding stiff and strong,
Though each was partly in the right,
    And all were in the wrong!

Moral

So oft in theologic wars,
    The disputants, I ween,
Rail on in utter ignorance
    Of what each other mean,
And prate about an Elephant
    Not one of them has seen!

The Elephant

Hilaire Belloc

When people call this beast to mind,
They marvel more and more
    At such a LITTLE tail behind,
So LARGE a trunk before.

The Yak

Hilaire Belloc

As a friend to the children
Commend me the Yak.
You will find it exactly the thing:
It will carry and fetch, you can ride on its back,
Or lead it about with a string.

The Tartar who dwells on the plains of Thibet
(A desolate region of snow)
Has for centuries made it a nursery pet,
And surely the Tartar should know!
Then tell you papa where the Yak can be got,
And if he is awfully rich
He will buy you the creature—
or else
he will not.
(I cannot be positive which.)

The Platypus

Oliver Herford

My child, the Duck-billed Platypus
A sad example sets for us.
From him we learn how Indecision
Of character provokes Derision.
This vacillating thing, you see,
Could not decide which he would be—
Fish, Flesh or Fowl,—and chose all three.
The scientists were sorely vexed,
To classify him so perplexed
Their brains that they with rage at bay
Called him a horrid name one day,
A name that baffles, frights and shocks us,
Ornithorynchus Paradoxus.

The Raven

Edgar Allan Poe

Once upon a midnight dreary, while I pondered, weak
and weary,
Over many a quaint and curious volume of forgotten lore,
While I nodded, nearly napping, suddenly there came a
tapping,
As of some one gently rapping, rapping at my chamber
door.
"'Tis some visitor," I muttered, "tapping at my chamber
door—
Only this, and nothing more."

Ah, distinctly I remember it was in the bleak December,
And each separate dying ember wrought its ghost upon the
floor.
Eagerly I wished the morrow;—vainly I had sought to
borrow
From my books surcease of sorrow—sorrow for the lost
Lenore—
For the rare and radiant maiden whom the angels name
Lenore—
Nameless here for evermore.

And the silken sad uncertain rustling of each purple
    curtain
Thrilled me—filled me with fantastic terrors never felt
    before;
    So that now, to still the beating of my heart, I stood
        repeating,
    " 'Tis some visitor entreating entrance at my chamber
        door—
Some late visitor entreating entrance at my chamber
    door;—
            This it is, and nothing more."

  Presently my soul grew stronger; hesitating then no
    longer,
"Sir," said I, "or Madam, truly your forgiveness I implore;
    But the fact is I was napping, and so gently you came
        rapping,
    And so faintly you came tapping, tapping at my chamber
    door,
That I scarce was sure I heard you"—here I opened wide
    the door;—
            Darkness there, and nothing more.

  Deep into that darkness peering, long I stood there
    wondering, fearing,
Doubting, dreaming dreams no mortals ever dared to
    dream before;
    But the silence was unbroken, and the stillness gave no
    token,

And the only word there spoken was the whispered
        word, "Lenore!"
This I whispered, and an echo murmured back the word,
        "Lenore!"—
                    Merely this, and nothing more.

Back into the chamber turning, all my soul within me
        burning,
Soon again I heard a tapping somewhat louder than before.
        "Surely," said I, "surely that is something at my
            window lattice:
        Let me see, then, what thereat is, and this mystery
            explore—
Let my heart be still a moment and this mystery explore;—
                    'Tis the wind and nothing more."

Open here I flung the shutter, when, with many a flirt
        and flutter,
In there stepped a stately raven of the saintly days of yore;
        Not the least obeisance made he; not a minute stopped
            or stayed he;
        But, with mien of lord or lady, perched above my
            chamber door—
Perched upon a bust of Pallas just above my chamber
        door—
                    Perched, and sat, and nothing more.

Then this ebony bird beguiling my sad fancy into smiling,
By the grave and stern decorum of the countenance it wore,
    "Though thy crest be shorn and shaven, thou," I said,
        "art sure no craven,
    Ghastly grim and ancient raven wandering from the
        Nightly shore—
Tell me what thy lordly name is on the Night's Plutonian
    shore!"
                    Quoth the Raven, "Nevermore."

    Much I marveled this ungainly fowl to hear discourse so
        plainly
Though its answer little meaning—little relevancy bore;
    For we cannot help agreeing that no living human being
    Ever yet was blest with seeing bird above his chamber
        door—
Bird or beast upon the sculptured bust above his chamber
    door,
                    With such name as "Nevermore."

    But the raven, sitting lonely on the placid bust, spoke only
That one word, as if his soul in that one word he did
    outpour.
    Nothing further then he uttered—not a feather then he
        fluttered—
    Till I scarcely more than muttered, "Other friends have
        flown before—
On the morrow *he* will leave me, as my hopes have flown
    before."
                    Then the bird said, "Nevermore."

Startled at the stillness broken by reply so aptly spoken,
"Doubtless," said I, "what it utters is its only stock and
store,
    Caught from some unhappy master whom unmerciful
Disaster
    Followed fast and followed faster till his songs one
burden bore—
Till the dirges of his Hope that melancholy burden bore
        Of 'Never—nevermore.' "

But the Raven still beguiling all my fancy into smiling,
Straight I wheeled a cushioned seat in front of bird, and
bust and door;
    Then upon the velvet sinking, I betook myself to linking
    Fancy unto fancy, thinking what this ominous bird of
yore—
What this grim, ungainly, ghastly, gaunt and ominous bird
of yore
        Meant in croaking "Nevermore."

This I sat engaged in guessing, but no syllable expressing
To the fowl whose fiery eyes now burned into my bosom's
core;
    This and more I sat divining, with my head at ease
reclining
    On the cushion's velvet lining that the lamplight gloated
o'er,
But whose velvet violet lining with the lamplight gloating
o'er,
        She shall press, ah, nevermore!

Then methought the air grew denser, perfumed from an
   unseen censer
Swung by Seraphim whose footfalls tinkled on the tufted
   floor.
   "Wretch," I cried, "thy God hath lent thee—by these
      angels he hath sent thee
   Respite—respite and nepenthe, from thy memories of
      Lenore!
Quaff, oh quaff this kind nepenthe and forget this lost
   Lenore!"
               Quoth the Raven, "Nevermore."

   "Prophet!" said I, "thing of evil!—prophet still, if bird or
      devil!—
Whether Tempter sent, or whether tempest tossed thee
   here ashore,
   Desolate yet all undaunted, on this desert land
      enchanted—
   On this home by horror haunted—tell me truly, I
      implore—
Is there—*is* there balm in Gilead?—tell me—tell me, I
   implore!"
               Quoth the Raven, "Nevermore."

   "Prophet!" said I, "thing of evil—prophet still, if bird or
      devil!
By that Heaven that bends above us—by that God we both
   adore—
   Tell this soul with sorrow laden if, within the distant
      Aidenn,

It shall clasp a sainted maiden whom the angels name
    Lenore—
Clasp a rare and radiant maiden whom the angels name
    Lenore."
            Quoth the Raven, "Nevermore."

"Be that word our sign in parting, bird or fiend," I
    shrieked, upstarting—
"Get thee back into the tempest and the Night's Plutonian
    shore!
    Leave no black plume as a token of that lie thy soul hath
        spoken!
    Leave my loneliness unbroken!—quit the bust above my
        door!
Take thy beak from out my heart, and take thy form from
    off my door!"
            Quoth the Raven, "Nevermore."

And the Raven, never flitting, still is sitting, still is sitting
On the pallid bust of Pallas just above my chamber door;
    And his eyes have all the seeming of a demon's that is
        dreaming,
    And the lamplight o'er him streaming throws his shadow
        on the floor;
And my soul from out that shadow that lies floating on the
    floor
            Shall be lifted—nevermore!

Old Pond

Bashō

Old pond—
A frog leaps in—
Water's sound.

Don't Kill That Fly!

Kobayashi Issa

Look, don't kill that fly!
It is making a prayer to you
By rubbing its hands and feet.

The Itsy Bitsy Spider

Anonymous

The itsy bitsy spider went up the water spout.
Down came the rain, and washed the spider out.
Out came the sun, and dried up all the rain,
And the itsy bitsy spider went up the spout again.

A Noiseless Patient Spider

Walt Whitman

A noiseless patient spider,
I mark'd where on a little promontory it stood isolated,
Mark'd how to explore the vacant vast surrounding,
It launch'd forth filament, filament, filament, out of itself,
Ever unreeling them, ever tirelessly speeding them.

And you O my soul where you stand,
Surrounded, detached, in measureless oceans of space,
Ceaselessly musing, venturing, throwing, seeking the
    spheres to connect them,
Till the bridge you will need be form'd, till the ductile
    anchor hold,
Till the gossamer thread you fling catch somewhere,
    O my soul.

The Pied Piper of Hamelin

A CHILD'S STORY

Robert Browning

(Written for, and Inscribed to, W. M. the Younger)

1

Hamelin Town's in Brunswick,
  By famous Hanover city;
The river Weser, deep and wide,
Washes its wall on the southern side;
A pleasanter spot you never spied;
  But, when begins my ditty,
Almost five hundred years ago,
To see the townsfolk suffer so
  From vermin, was a pity.

2

  Rats!
They fought the dogs and killed the cats,
  And bit the babies in the cradles,
And ate the cheeses out of the vats,
  And licked the soup from the cooks' own ladles,
Split open the kegs of salted sprats,
Made nests inside men's Sunday hats,
And even spoiled the women's chats
    By drowning their speaking
    With shrieking and squeaking
In fifty different sharps and flats.

3

At last the people in a body
　　To the Town Hall came flocking:
"'T is clear," cried they, "our Mayor's a noddy;
　　And as for our Corporation—shocking
To think we buy gowns lined with ermine
For dolts that can't or won't determine
What's best to rid us of our vermin!
You hope, because you're old and obese,
To find in the furry civic robe ease?
Rouse up, sirs! Give your brains a racking
To find the remedy we're lacking,
Or, sure as fate, we'll send you packing!"
At this the Mayor and Corporation
Quaked with a mighty consternation.

4

An hour they sat in council,
　　At length the Mayor broke silence:
"For a guilder I'd my ermine gown sell,
　　I wish I were a mile hence!
It's easy to bid one rack one's brain—
I'm sure my poor head aches again,
I've scratched it so, and all in vain.
Oh for a trap, a trap, a trap!"
Just as he said this, what should hap
At the chamber door but a gentle tap?
"Bless us," cried the Mayor, "what's that?"
(With the Corporation as he sat,

Looking little though wondrous fat;
Nor brighter was his eye, nor moister
Than a too-long-opened oyster,
Save when at noon his paunch grew mutinous
For a plate of turtle green and glutinous)
"Only a scraping of shoes on the mat?
Anything like the sound of a rat
Makes my heart go pit-a-pat!"

5

"Come in!"—the Mayor cried, looking bigger:
And in did come the strangest figure!
His queer long coat from heel to head
Was half of yellow and half of red,
And he himself was tall and thin,
With sharp blue eyes, each like a pin,
And light loose hair, yet swarthy skin,
No tuft on cheek nor beard on chin,
But lips where smiles went out and in;
There was no guessing his kith and kin:
And nobody could enough admire
The tall man and his quaint attire.
Quoth one: "It's as my great-grandsire,
Starting up at the Trump of Doom's tone,
Had walked this way from his painted tombstone!"

6

He advanced to the council-table:
And, "Please your honors," said he, "I'm able,
By means of a secret charm, to draw
    All creatures living beneath the sun,
    That creep or swim or fly or run,
After me so as you never saw!
And I chiefly use my charm
On creatures that do people harm,
The mole and toad and newt and viper;
And people call me the Pied Piper."
(And here they noticed round his neck
    A scarf of red and yellow stripe,
To match with his coat of the self-same check;
    And at the scarf's end hung a pipe;
And his fingers, they noticed, were ever straying
As if impatient to be playing
Upon this pipe, as low it dangled
Over his vesture so old-fangled.)
"Yet," said he, "poor piper as I am,
In Tartary I freed the Cham,
    Last June, from his huge swarms of gnats;
I eased in Asia the Nizam
    Of a monstrous brood of vampyre-bats:
And as for what your brain bewilders,
    If I can rid your town of rats
Will you give me a thousand guilders?"
"One? fifty thousand!"—was the exclamation
Of the astonished Mayor and Corporation.

Into the street the Piper stept,
    Smiling first a little smile,
As if he knew what magic slept
    In his quiet pipe the while;
Then, like a musical adept,
To blow the pipe his lips he wrinkled,
And green and blue his sharp eyes twinkled,
Like a candle-flame where salt is sprinkled;
And ere three shrill notes the pipe uttered,
You heard as if an army muttered;
And the muttering grew to a grumbling;
And the grumbling grew to a mighty rumbling;
And out of the houses the rats came tumbling.
Great rats, small rats, lean rats, brawny rats,
Brown rats, black rats, gray rats, tawny rats,
Grave old plodders, gay young friskers,
    Fathers, mothers, uncles, cousins,
Cocking tails and pricking whiskers,
    Families by tens and dozens,
Brothers, sisters, husbands, wives—
Followed the Piper for their lives.
From street to street he piped advancing,
And step for step they followed dancing,
Until they came to the river Weser,
    Wherein all plunged and perished!
—Save one who, stout as Julius Cæsar,
Swam across and lived to carry
    (As he, the manuscript he cherished)
To Rat-land home his commentary:

Which was, "At the first shrill notes of the pipe,
I heard a sound as of scraping tripe,
And putting apples, wondrous ripe,
Into a cider-press's gripe:
And a moving away of pickle-tub-boards,
And a leaving ajar of conserve-cupboards,
And a drawing the corks of train-oil-flasks,
And a breaking the hoops of butter-casks:
And it seemed as if a voice
   (Sweeter far than by harp or by psaltery
Is breathed) called out, 'Oh rats, rejoice!
   The world is grown to one vast drysaltery!
So munch on, crunch on, take your nuncheon,
Breakfast, supper, dinner, luncheon!'
And just as a bulky sugar-puncheon,
All ready staved, like a great sun shone
Glorious scarce an inch before me,
Just as methought it said, 'Come, bore me!'
—I found the Weser rolling o'er me."

8

You should have heard the Hamelin people
Ringing the bells till they rocked the steeple.
"Go," cried the Mayor, "and get long poles,
Poke out the nests and block up the holes!
Consult with carpenters and builders,
And leave in our town not even a trace
Of the rats!"—when suddenly, up the face
Of the Piper perked in the market-place,
With a, "First, if you please, my thousand guilders!"

9

A thousand guilders! The Mayor looked blue;
So did the Corporation too.
For council dinners made rare havoc
With Claret, Moselle, Vin-de-Grave, Hock;
And half the money would replenish
Their cellar's biggest butt with Rhenish.
To pay this sum to a wandering fellow
With a gypsy coat of red and yellow!
"Beside, quoth the Mayor with a knowing wink,
"Our business was done at the river's brink;
We saw with our eyes the vermin sink,
And what's dead can't come to life, I think.
So, friend, we're not the folks to shrink
From the duty of giving you something for drink,
And a matter of money to put in your poke;
But as for the guilders, what we spoke
Of them, as you very well know, was in joke.
Beside, our losses have made us thrifty.
A thousand guilders! Come, take fifty!"

10

The Piper's face fell, and he cried
"No trifling! I can't wait, beside!
I've promised to visit by dinnertime
Bagdat, and accept the prime
Of the Head-Cook's pottage, all he's rich in,
For having left, in the Caliph's kitchen,
Of a nest of scorpions no survivor:
With him I proved no bargain-driver,

With you, don't think I'll bate a stiver!
And folks who put me in a passion
May find me pipe after another fashion."

11

"How?" cried the Mayor, "d'ye think I brook
Being worse treated than a Cook?
Insulted by a lazy ribald
With idle pipe and vesture piebald?
You theaten us, fellow? Do your worst,
Blow your pipe there till you burst!"

12

Once more he stept into the street
   And to his lips again
   Laid his long pipe of smooth straight cane;
And ere he blew three notes (such sweet
Soft notes as yet musician's cunning
   Never gave the enraptured air)
There was a rustling that seemed like a bustling
Of merry crowds justling at pitching and hustling,
Small feet were pattering, wooden shoes clattering,
Little hands clapping and little tongues chattering,
And, like fowls in a farm-yard when barley is scattering,
Out came the children running.
All the little boys and girls,
With rosy cheeks and flaxen curls,
And sparkling eyes and teeth like pearls,
Tripping and skipping, ran merrily after
The wonderful music with shouting and laughter.

13

The Mayor was dumb, and the Council stood
As if they were changed into blocks of wood.
Unable to move a step, or cry
To the children merrily skipping by,
—Could only follow with the eye
That joyous crowd at the Piper's back.
But how the Mayor was on the rack,
And the wretched Council's bosoms beat,
As the Piper turned from the High Street
To where the Weser rolled its waters
Right in the way of their sons and daughters!
However he turned from South to West,
And to Koppelberg Hill his steps addressed,
And after him the children pressed;
Great was the joy in every breast.
"He never can cross that mighty top!
He's forced to let the piping drop,
And we shall see our children stop!"
When, lo, as they reached the mountain-side,
A wondrous portal opened wide,
As if a cavern was suddenly hollowed;
And the Piper advanced and the children followed,
And when all were in to the very last,
The door in the mountain-side shut fast.
Did I say, all? No! One was lame,
     And could not dance the whole of the way;
And in after years, if you would blame
     His sadness, he was used to say,—
"It's dull in our town since my playmates left!

I can't forget that I'm bereft
Of all the pleasant sights they see,
Which the Piper also promised me.
For he led us, he said, to a joyous land,
Joining the town and just at hand,
Where waters gushed and fruit-trees grew
And flowers put forth a fairer hue,
And everything was strange and new;
The sparrows were brighter than peacocks here,
And their dogs outran our fallow deer,
And honey-bees had lost their stings,
And horses were born with eagles' wings:
And just as I became assured
My lame foot would be speedily cured,
The music stopped and I stood still,
And found myself outside the hill,
Left alone against my will,
To go now limping as before,
And never hear of that country more!"

14

Alas, alas for Hamelin!
   There came into many a burgher's pate
   A text which says that heaven's gate
   Opes to the rich at as easy rate
As the needle's eye takes a camel in!
The mayor sent East, West, North and South,
To offer the Piper, by word of mouth,
   Wherever it was men's lot to find him,
Silver and gold to his heart's content,

If he'd only return the way he went,
    And bring the children behind him.
But when they saw't was a lost endeavor,
And Piper and dancers were gone for ever,
They made a decree that lawyers never
    Should think their records dated duly
If, after the day of the month and year,
These words did not as well appear,
"And so long after what happened here
    On the Twenty-second of July,
Thirteen hundred and seventy-six":
And the better in memory to fix
The place of the children's last retreat,
They called it, the Pied Piper's Street—
Where any one playing on pipe or tabor
Was sure for the future to lose his labor.
Nor suffered they hostelry or tavern
    To shock with mirth a street so solemn;
But opposite the place of the cavern
    They wrote the story on a column,
And on the great church-window painted
The same, to make the world acquainted
How their children were stolen away,
And there it stands to this very day.
And I must not omit to say
That in Transylvania there's a tribe
Of alien people who ascribe
The outlandish ways and dress
On which their neighbors lay such stress,
To their fathers and mothers having risen

Out of some subterraneous prison
Into which they were trepanned
Long time ago in a mighty band
Out of Hamelin town in Brunswick land,
But how or why, they don't understand.

15

So, Willy, let me and you be wipers
Of scores out with all men—especially pipers!
And, whether they pipe us free from rats or from mice,
If we've promised them aught, let us keep our promise!

A Wise Old Owl

Anonymous

A wise old owl sat in an oak,
The more he heard, the less he spoke;
The less he spoke, the more he heard;
Why aren't we all like that wise old bird?

FUN TO READ
ALOUD

One of the things that makes a poem a poem is the actual sound of the words and the rhythm (or meter) that carries the words along. Sometimes the beat of a poem and the way its words rhyme make it seem more like a song than anything else, and the best way to enjoy a song is to sing it! Some of these poems were meant to be recited to an audience, whether small or large— "A Visit from St. Nicholas" is a great example—but others, like "Kubla Khan" or "The Bells" or "Fuzzy Wuzzy" sound great even if you're just listening to the words in your head as you read them to yourself. The ideas in poems are often very powerful, but it's the sound the words make when you listen to them that makes them poetry.

Kubla Khan

OR A VISION IN A DREAM. A FRAGMENT

Samuel Taylor Coleridge

In Xanadu did Kubla Khan
A stately pleasure dome decree:
Where Alph, the sacred river, ran
Through caverns measureless to man
   Down to a sunless sea.
So twice five miles of fertile ground
With walls and towers were girdled round:
And there were gardens bright with sinuous rills,
Where blossomed many an incense-bearing tree;
And here were forests ancient as the hills,
Enfolding sunny spots of greenery.

But oh! that deep romantic chasm which slanted
Down the green hill athwart a cedarn cover!
A savage place! as holy and enchanted
As e'er beneath a waning moon was haunted
By woman wailing for her demon lover!
And from this chasm, with ceaseless turmoil seething,
As if this earth in fast thick pants were breathing,
A mighty fountain momently was forced:
Amid whose swift half-intermitted burst
Huge fragments vaulted like rebounding hail,
Or chaffy grain beneath the thresher's flail:
And 'mid these dancing rocks at once and ever

It flung up momently the sacred river.
Five miles meandering with a mazy motion
Through wood and dale the sacred river ran,
Then reached the caverns measureless to man,
And sank in tumult to a lifeless ocean:
And 'mid this tumult Kubla heard from far
Ancestral voices prophesying war!

The shadow of the dome of pleasure
Floated midway on the waves;
Where was heard the mingled measure
From the fountain and the caves.
It was a miracle of rare device,
A sunny pleasure dome with caves of ice!

A damsel with a dulcimer
In a vision once I saw:
It was an Abyssinian maid,
And on her dulcimer she played,
Singing of Mount Abora.
Could I revive within me
Her symphony and song,
To such a deep delight 'twould win me,
That with music loud and long,
I would build that dome in air,
That sunny dome! those caves of ice!
And all who heard should see them there,
And all should cry, Beware! Beware!
His flashing eyes, his floating hair!

Weave a circle round him thrice,
And close your eyes with holy dread,
For he on honey-dew hath fed,
And drunk the milk of Paradise.

A Visit from St. Nicholas

Clement Clarke Moore

'Twas the night before Christmas, when all through the
    house
Not a creature was stirring, not even a mouse;
The stockings were hung by the chimney with care,
In hopes that St. Nicholas soon would be there;
The children were nestled all snug in their beds,
While visions of sugar-plums danced in their heads;
And mamma in her 'kerchief, and I in my cap,
Had just settled our brains for a long winter's nap—
When out on the lawn there arose such a clatter,
I sprang from my bed to see what was the matter.
Away to the window I flew like a flash,
Tore open the shutters, and threw up the sash.
The moon, on the breast of the new-fallen snow,
Gave the lustre of midday to objects below;
When, what to my wondering eyes should appear,
But a miniature sleigh and eight tiny reindeer,
With a little old driver, so lively and quick,
I knew in a moment it must be St. Nick.
More rapid than eagles his coursers they came,
And he whistled, and shouted, and called them by name:
"Now, Dasher! now, Dancer! now, Prancer and Vixen!
On, Comet! on, Cupid! on, Donder and Blitzen!
To the top of the porch! to the top of the wall!

Now dash away! dash away! dash away all!"
As dry leaves that before the wild hurricane fly,
When they meet with an obstacle, mount to the sky;
So up to the house-top the coursers they flew
With the sleigh full of toys, and St. Nicholas too.
And then, in a twinkling, I heard on the roof
The prancing and pawing of each little hoof—
As I drew in my head, and was turning around,
Down the chimney St. Nicholas came with a bound.
He was dressed all in fur, from his head to his foot,
And his clothes were all tarnished with ashes and soot;
A bundle of toys he had flung on his back,
And he looked like a peddler just opening his pack.
His eyes—how they twinkled; his dimples, how merry!
His cheeks were like roses, his nose like a cherry!
His droll little mouth was drawn up like a bow,
And the beard of his chin was as white as the snow;
The stump of a pipe he held tight in his teeth,
And the smoke it encircled his head like a wreath;
He had a broad face and a little round belly
That shook, when he laughed, like a bowl full of jelly.
He was chubby and plump, a right jolly old elf,
And I laughed when I saw him, in spite of myself;
A wink of his eye and a twist of his head
Soon gave me to know I had nothing to dread;
He spoke not a word, but went straight to his work,
And filled all the stockings; then turned with a jerk,
And laying his finger aside of his nose,
And giving a nod, up the chimney he rose;

He sprang to his sleigh, to his team gave a whistle,
And away they all flew like the down of a thistle.
But I heard him exclaim, ere he drove out of sight,
"Happy Christmas to all, and to all a good night!"

The Boy Who Laughed at Santa Claus

Ogden Nash

In Baltimore there lived a boy.
He wasn't anybody's joy.
Although his name was Jabez Dawes,
His character was full of flaws.
In school he never led his classes,
He hid old ladies' reading glasses.
His mouth was open when he chewed,
And elbows to the table glued.

He stole the milk of hungry kittens,
And walked through doors marked No ADMITTANCE.
He said he acted thus because
There wasn't any Santa Claus.
Another trick that tickled Jabez
Was crying "Boo!" at little babies.
He brushed his teeth, they said in town,
Sideways instead of up and down.

Yet people pardoned every sin,
And viewed his antics with a grin,
Till they were told by Jabez Dawes,
"There isn't any Santa Claus!"

Deploring how he did behave,
His parents swiftly sought their grave.
They hurried through the portals pearly,
And Jabez left the funeral early.

Like whooping cough, from child to child,
He sped to spread the rumor wild:
"Sure as my name is Jabez Dawes
There isn't any Santa Claus!"
Slunk like a weasel or a marten
Through nursery and kindergarten,
Whispering low to every tot,
"There isn't any, no there's not!

"No beard, no pipe, no scarlet clothes,
No twinkling eyes, no cherry nose,
No sleigh, and furthermore, by Jiminy,
Nobody coming down the chimney!"

The children wept all Christmas Eve
And Jabez chortled up his sleeve.
No infant dared to hang up his stocking
For fear of Jabez' ribald mocking.
He sprawled on his untidy bed,
Fresh malice dancing in his head,
When presently with scalp a-tingling,
Jabez heard a distant jingling;
He heard the crunch of sleigh and hoof
Crisply alighting on the roof.

What good to rise and bar the door?
A shower of soot was on the floor.
Jabez beheld, oh, awe of awes,
The fireplace full of Santa Claus!
Then Jabez fell upon his knees
With cries of "Don't," and "Pretty please."
He howled, "I don't know where you read it.
I swear some other fellow said it!"

"Jabez," replied the angry saint,
"It isn't I, it's you that ain't.
Although there is a Santa Claus,
There isn't any Jabez Dawes!"
Said Jabez then with impudent vim,
"Oh, yes there is; and I am him!
Your magic don't scare me, it doesn't"—
And suddenly he found he wasn't!

From grimy feet to unkempt locks
Jabez became a jack-in-the-box,
An ugly toy in Santa's sack,
Mounting the flue on Santa's back.
The neighbors heard his mournful squeal;
They searched for him, but not with zeal.
No trace was found of Jabez Dawes,
Which led to thunderous applause,
And people drank a loving cup
And went and hung their stockings up.

All you who sneer at Santa Claus,
Beware the fate of Jabez Dawes,
The saucy boy who mocked the saint,
Donder and Blitzen licked off his paint.

Eldorado

Edgar Allan Poe

Gaily bedight,
A gallant knight,
In sunshine and in shadow,
Had journeyed long,
Singing a song,
In search of Eldorado.

But he grew old—
This knight so bold—
And o'er his heart a shadow
Fell, as he found
No spot of ground
That looked like Eldorado.

And, as his strength
Failed him at length
He met a pilgrim shadow—
"Shadow," said he,
"Where can it be—
This land of Eldorado?"

"Over the Mountains
Of the Moon,
Down the Valley of the Shadow,
Ride, boldly ride,"
The shade replied,—
"If you seek for Eldorado!"

The Bells

Edgar Allan Poe

1

Hear the sledges with the bells—
Silver bells!
What a world of merriment their melody foretells!
How they tinkle, tinkle, tinkle,
In the icy air of night!
While the stars that oversprinkle
All the heavens, seem to twinkle
With a crystalline delight;
Keeping time, time, time,
In a sort of Runic rhyme,
To the tintinnabulation that so musically wells
From the bells, bells, bells, bells,
Bells, bells, bells—
From the jingling and the tinkling of the bells.

2

Hear the mellow wedding bells,
Golden bells!
What a world of happiness their harmony foretells!
Through the balmy air of night
How they ring out their delight!
From the molten-golden notes,
And all in tune,
What a liquid ditty floats

To the turtle-dove that listens, while she gloats
On the moon!
Oh, from out the sounding cells,
What a gush of euphony voluminously wells!
How it swells!
How it dwells
On the Future! how it tells
Of the rapture that impels
To the swinging and the ringing
Of the bells, bells, bells,
Of the bells, bells, bells, bells,
Bells, bells, bells—
To the rhyming and the chiming of the bells!

3

Hear the loud alarum bells—
Brazen bells!
What a tale of terror, now, their turbulency tells!
In the startled ear of night
How they scream out their affright!
Too much horrified to speak,
They can only shriek, shriek,
Out of tune,
In a clamorous appealing to the mercy of the fire,
In a mad expostulation with the deaf and frantic fire,
Leaping higher, higher, higher,
With a desperate desire,
And a resolute endeavor,
Now—now to sit or never,

By the side of the pale-faced moon.
Oh, the bells, bells, bells!
What a tale their terror tells
Of Despair!
How they clang, and clash, and roar!
What a horror they outpour
On the bosom of the palpitating air!
Yet the ear it fully knows,
By the twanging,
And the clanging,
How the danger ebbs and flows:
Yet the ear distinctly tells,
In the jangling,
And the wrangling,
How the danger sinks and swells,
By the sinking or the swelling in the anger of the bells—
Of the bells—
Of the bells, bells, bells, bells,
Bells, bells, bells—
In the clamor and the clanger of the bells!

4

Hear the tolling of the bells—
Iron bells!
What a world of solemn thought their monody compels!
In the silence of the night,
How we shiver with affright
At the melancholy menace of their tone!
For every sound that floats

From the rust within their throats
    Is a groan.
And the people—ah, the people—
They that dwell up in the steeple,
    All alone,
And who, tolling, tolling, tolling,
  In that muffled monotone,
Feel a glory in so rolling
  On the human heart a stone—
They are neither man nor woman—
They are neither brute nor human—
    They are Ghouls:
  And their king it is who tolls;
  And he rolls, rolls, rolls,
    Rolls
    A paean from the bells!
And his merry bosom swells
  With the paean of the bells!
And he dances, and he yells;
Keeping time, time, time,
In a sort of Runic rhyme,
  To the paean of the bells—
    Of the bells:
Keeping time, time, time,
In a sort of Runic rhyme,
  To the throbbing of the bells—
Of the bells, bells, bells—
  To the sobbing of the bells;
Keeping time, time, time,
  As he knells, knells, knells,

In a happy Runic rhyme,
    To the rolling of the bells—
Of the bells, bells, bells:
    To the tolling of the bells,
Of the bells, bells, bells, bells—
    Bells, bells, bells—
To the moaning and the groaning of the bells.

From The Song of Hiawatha

Henry Wadsworth Longfellow

By the shores of Gitche Gumee,
By the shining Big-Sea-Water,
Stood the wigwam of Nokomis,
Daughter of the Moon, Nokomis.
Dark behind it rose the forest,
Rose the black and gloomy pine-trees,
Rose the firs with cones upon them;
Bright before it beat the water,
Beat the clear and sunny water,
Beat the shining Big-Sea-Water.
 There the wrinkled old Nokomis
Nursed the little Hiawatha,
Rocked him in his linden cradle,
Bedded soft in moss and rushes,
Safely bound with reindeer sinews;
Stilled his fretful wail by saying,
"Hush! the Naked Bear will hear thee!"
Lulled him into slumber, singing,
"Ewa-yea! my little owlet!
Who is this, that lights the wigwam?
With his great eyes lights the wigwam?
Ewa-yea! my little owlet!"

The Modern Hiawatha

George A. Strong

He killed the noble Mudjokivis;
With the skin he made him mittens,
Made them with the fur side inside,
Made them with the skin side outside,
He, to get the warm side inside,
Put the inside skin side outside:
He, to get the cold side outside,
Put the warm side fur side inside:
That's why he put the fur side inside,
Why he put the skin side outside,
Why he turned them inside outside.

Fuzzy Wuzzy Was a Bear

Anonymous

Fuzzy Wuzzy was a bear.
Fuzzy Wuzzy had no hair.
Fuzzy Wuzzy wasn't fuzzy, was he?

The Fiddler of Dooney

William Butler Yeats

When I play on my fiddle in Dooney,
Folk dance like a wave of the sea;
My cousin is priest in Kilvarnet,
My brother in Moharabuiee.

I passed my brother and cousin:
They read in their books of prayer;
I read in my book of songs
I bought at the Sligo fair.

When we come at the end of time,
To Peter sitting in state,
He will smile on the three old spirits,
But call me first through the gate;

For the good are always the merry,
Save by an evil chance,
And the merry love the fiddle
And the merry love to dance:

And when the folk there spy me,
They will all come up to me,
With "Here is the fiddler of Dooney!"
And dance like a wave of the sea.

Wynken, Blynken, and Nod

Eugene Field

Wynken, Blynken, and Nod one night
   Sailed off in a wooden shoe—
Sailed on a river of crystal light,
   Into a sea of dew.
"Where are you going, and what do you wish?"
   The old moon asked the three.
   "We have come to fish for the herring fish
   That live in this beautiful sea;
   Nets of silver and gold have we!"
       Said Wynken,
       Blynken,
       And Nod.

The old moon laughed and sang a song,
   As they rocked in the wooden shoe,
And the wind that sped them all night long
   Ruffled the waves of dew.
The little stars were the herring fish
   That lived in that beautiful sea—
   "Now cast your nets wherever you wish—
   Never afeard are we";
   So cried the stars to the fishermen three:
       Wynken,
       Blynken,
       And Nod.

All night long their nets they threw
    To the stars in the twinkling foam—
Then down from the skies came the wooden shoe,
    Bringing the fishermen home;
'T was all so pretty a sail it seemed
    As if it could not be,
And some folks thought 'twas a dream they'd dreamed
    Of sailing that beautiful sea—
    But I shall name you the fishermen three:
            Wynken,
            Blynken,
            And Nod.

Wynken and Blynken are two little eyes,
    And Nod is a little head,
And the wooden shoe that sailed the skies
    Is the wee one's trundle-bed.
So shut your eyes while mother sings
    Of wonderful sights that be,
And you shall see the beautiful things
    As you rock in the misty sea,
    Where the old shoe rocked the fishermen three:
            Wynken,
            Blynken,
            And Nod.

What Are Little Boys Made Of?

Anonymous

What are little boys made of?
What are little boys made of?
   Frogs and snails
   And puppy-dogs' tails,
That's what little boys are made of.

What are little girls made of?
What are little girls made of?
   Sugar and spice
   And all that's nice,
That's what little girls are made of.

Monday's Child

Anonymous

Monday's child is fair of face,
Tuesday's child is full of grace,
Wednesday's child is full of woe,
Thursday's child has far to go,
Friday's child is loving and giving,
Saturday's child works hard for his living,
And the child that is born on the Sabbath day
Is bonny and blithe, and good and gay.

I'm Nobody! Who Are You?

Emily Dickinson

I'm Nobody! Who are you?
Are you — Nobody — too?
Then there's a pair of us!
Dont tell! they'd banish us — you know!

How dreary — to be — Somebody!
How public — like a Frog —
To tell your name — the livelong June —
To an admiring Bog!

Block City

Robert Louis Stevenson

What are you able to build with your blocks?
Castles and palaces, temples and docks.
Rain may keep raining, and others go roam,
But I can be happy and building at home.

Let the sofa be mountains, the carpet be sea,
There I'll establish a city for me:
A kirk and a mill and a palace beside,
And a harbor as well where my vessels may ride.

Great is the palace with pillar and wall,
A sort of a tower on the top of it all,
And steps coming down in an orderly way
To where my toy vessels lie safe in the bay.

This one is sailing and that one is moored:
Hark to the song of the sailors on board!
And see on the steps of my palace, the kings
Coming and going with presents and things!

Now I have done with it, down let it go!
All in a moment the town is laid low.
Block upon block lying scattered and free,
What is there left of my town by the sea?

Yet as I saw it, I see it again,
The kirk and the palace, the ships and the men,
And as long as I live and where'er I may be,
I'll always remember my town by the sea.

BATTLEFIELDS
AND HEROES

The great Confederate general Robert E. Lee was quoted as saying, "It is good that war is so horrible, or we might grow to like it." One thing is for sure: war makes for wonderful poems. Probably the main reason is that war creates the opportunities for heroes to perform great deeds for a larger cause, at the potential cost of their lives, and that kind of drama gives life to poetry. But dramatic situations aside, war poems just seem to sound exciting, perhaps because they are usually quick paced, like marching songs. The combination of heroism and powerful rhythms is a formula for great poetry, though sometimes the poems are not about triumphing against all odds, but, like "The Battle of Blenheim," about the horror and cost of war that General Lee recognized.

Paul Revere's Ride

Henry Wadsworth Longfellow

Listen, my children, and you shall hear
Of the midnight ride of Paul Revere,
On the eighteenth of April, in Seventy-five;
Hardly a man is now alive
Who remembers that famous day and year.

He said to his friend, "If the British march
By land or sea from the town to-night,
Hang a lantem aloft in the belfry arch
Of the North Church tower as a signal light,—
One, if by land, and two, if by sea;
And I on the opposite shore will be,
Ready to ride and spread the alarm
Through every Middlesex village and farm,
For the country folk to be up and to arm."

Then he said, "Goodnight!" and with muffled oar
Silently rowed to the Charlestown shore,
Just as the moon rose over the bay,
Where swinging wide at her moorings lay
The *Somerset*, British man-of-war;
A phantom ship, with each mast and spar
Across the moon like a prison bar,
And a huge black hulk, that was magnified
By its own reflection in the tide.

Meanwhile, his friend, through alley and street,
Wanders and watches with eager ears,
Till in the silence around him he hears
The muster of men at the barrack door,
The sound of arms, and the tramp of feet,
And the measured tread of the grenadiers,
Marching down to their boats on the shore.

Then he climbed the tower of the Old North Church,
By the wooden stairs, with stealthy tread,
To the belfry-chamber overhead,
And startled the pigeons from their perch
On the somber rafters, that round him made
Masses and moving shapes of shade,—
By the trembling ladder, steep and tall,
To the highest window in the wall,
Where he paused to listen and look down
A moment on the roofs of the town,
And the moonlight flowing over all.

Beneath, in the churchyard, lay the dead,
In their night-encampment on the hill,
Wrapped in silence so deep and still
That he could hear, like a sentinel's tread,
The watchful night-wind, as it went
Creeping along from tent to tent,
And seeming to whisper, "All is well!"
A moment only he feels the spell
Of the place and the hour, and the secret dread

Of the lonely belfry and the dead;
For suddenly all his thoughts are bent
On a shadowy something far away,
Where the river widens to meet the bay,—
A line of black that bends and floats
On the rising tide, like a bridge of boats.

Meanwhile, impatient to mount and ride,
Booted and spurred, with a heavy stride
On the opposite shore walked Paul Revere.
Now he patted his horse's side,
Now gazed at the landscape far and near,
Then, impetuous, stamped the earth,
And turned and tightened his saddle-girth;
But mostly he watched with eager search
The belfry-tower of the Old North Church,
As it rose above the graves on the hill,
Lonely and spectral and somber and still.
And lo! as he looks, on the belfry's height
A glimmer, and then a gleam of light!
He springs to the saddle, the bridle he turns,
But lingers and gazes, till full on his sight
A second lamp in the belfry burns!

A hurry of hoofs in a village street,
A shape in the moonlight, a bulk in the dark,
And beneath, from the pebbles, in passing, a spark
Struck out by a steed flying fearless and fleet:
That was all! And yet, through the gloom and the light,

The fate of a nation was riding that night;
And the spark struck out by that steed, in his flight,
Kindled the land into flame with its heat.

He has left the village and mounted the steep,
And beneath him, tranquil and broad and deep,
Is the Mystic, meeting the ocean tides;
And under the alders that skirt its edge,
Now soft on the sand, now loud on the ledge,
Is heard the tramp of his steed as he rides.

It was twelve by the village clock,
When he crossed the bridge into Medford town.
He heard the crowing of the cock,
And the barking of the farmer's dog,
And felt the damp of the river fog,
That rises after the sun goes down.

It was one by the village clock,
When he galloped into Lexington.
He saw the gilded weathercock
Swim in the moonlight as he passed,
And the meeting-house windows, blank and bare,
Gaze at him with a spectral glare,
As if they already stood aghast
At the bloody work they would look upon.

It was two by the village clock,
When he came to the bridge in Concord town.
He heard the bleating of the flock,

And the twitter of birds among the trees,
And felt the breath of the morning breeze
Blowing over the meadows brown.
And one was safe and asleep in his bed
Who at the bridge would be first to fall,
Who that day would be lying dead,
Pierced by a British musket-ball.

You know the rest. In the books you have read,
How the British Regulars fired and fled,—
How the farmers gave them ball for ball,
From behind each fence and farm-yard wall,
Chasing the red-coats down the lane,
Then crossing the fields to emerge again
Under the trees at the turn of the road,
And only pausing to fire and load.

So through the night rode Paul Revere;
And so through the night went his cry of alarm
To every Middlesex village and farm,—
A cry of defiance and not of fear,
A voice in the darkness, a knock at the door,
And a word that shall echo forevermore!
For, borne on the night-wind of the Past,
Through all our history, to the last,
In the hour of darkness and peril and need,
The people will waken and listen to hear
The hurrying hoof-beats of that steed,
And the midnight message of Paul Revere.

Old Ironsides

Oliver Wendell Holmes

Ay, tear her tattered ensign down!
   Long has it waved on high,
And many an eye has danced to see
   That banner in the sky;
Beneath it rung the battle shout,
   And burst the cannon's roar;—
The meteor of the ocean air
   Shall sweep the clouds no more.

Her deck, once red with heroes' blood,
   Where knelt the vanquished foe,
When winds were hurrying o'er the flood,
   And waves were white below,
No more shall feel the victor's tread,
   Or know the conquered knee;—
The harpies of the shore shall pluck
   The eagle of the sea!

O better that her shattered hulk
   Should sink beneath the wave;
Her thunders shook the mighty deep,
   And there should be her grave;
Nail to the mast her holy flag,
   Set every thread-bare sail,
And give her to the god of storms,—
   The lightning and the gale!

Concord Hymn

Ralph Waldo Emerson

By the rude bridge that arched the flood,
　　Their flag to April's breeze unfurled,
Here once the embattled farmers stood
　　And fired the shot heard round the world.

The foe long since in silence slept;
　　Alike the conqueror silent sleeps;
And Time the ruined bridge has swept
　　Down the dark stream which seaward creeps.

On this green bank, by this soft stream,
　　We set to-day a votive stone;
That memory may their deed redeem,
　　When, like our sires, our sons are gone.

Spirit, that made those heroes dare
　　To die, and leave their children free,
Bid Time and Nature gently spare
　　The shaft we raise to them and thee.

Barbara Frietchie

John Greenleaf Whittier

Up from the meadows rich with corn,
Clear in the cool September morn,

The clustered spires of Frederick stand
Green-walled by the hills of Maryland.

Round about them orchards sweep,
Apple and peach trees fruited deep,

Fair as the garden of the Lord
To the eyes of the famished rebel horde,

On that pleasant morn of the early fall
When Lee marched over the mountain-wall;

Over the mountains winding down,
Horse and foot, into Frederick town.

Forty flags with their silver stars,
Forty flags with their crimson bars,

Flapped in the morning wind: the sun
Of noon looked down, and saw not one.

Up rose old Barbara Frietchie then,
Bowed with her fourscore years and ten;

Bravest of all in Frederick town,
She took up the flag the men hauled down;

In her attic window the staff she set,
To show that one heart was loyal yet.

Up the street came the rebel tread,
Stonewall Jackson riding ahead.

Under his slouched hat left and right
He glanced; the old flag met his sight.

"Halt!"—the dust-brown ranks stood fast.
"Fire!"—out blazed the rifle-blast.

It shivered the window, pane and sash;
It rent the banner with seam and gash.

Quick, as it fell, from the broken staff
Dame Barbara snatched the silken scarf.

She leaned far out on the window-sill,
And shook it forth with a royal will.

"Shoot, if you must, this old gray head,
But spare your country's flag," she said.

A shade of sadness, a blush of shame,
Over the face of the leader came;

The nobler nature within him stirred
To life at that woman's deed and word;

"Who touches a hair of yon gray head
Dies like a dog! March on!" he said.

All day long through Frederick street
Sounded the tread of marching feet:

All day long that free flag tost
Over the heads of the rebel host.

Ever its torn folds rose and fell
On the loyal winds that loved it well;

And through the hill-gaps sunset light
Shone over it with a warm good-night.

Barbara Frietchie's work is o'er,
And the Rebel rides on his raids no more.

Honor to her! and let a tear
Fall, for her sake, on Stonewall's bier.

Over Barbara Frietchie's grave,
Flag of Freedom and Union, wave!

Peace and order and beauty draw
Round thy symbol of light and law;

And ever the stars above look down
On thy stars below in Frederick town!

The Battle Hymn of the Republic

Julia Ward Howe

Mine eyes have seen the glory of the coming of the Lord:
He is trampling out the vintage where the grapes of wrath
    are stored;
He hath loosed the fatal lightning of His terrible swift
    sword:
      His truth is marching on.

I have seen Him in the watch-fires of a hundred circling
    camps,
They have builded Him an altar in the evening dews and
    damps;
I can read His righteous sentence by the dim and flaring
    lamps:
      His day is marching on.

I have read a fiery gospel writ in burnished rows of steel:
"As ye deal with my contemners, so with you my grace shall
    deal;
Let the Hero, born of woman, crush the serpent with his
    heel,
      Since God is marching on."

He has sounded forth the trumpet that shall never call
    retreat;
He is sifting out the hearts of men before His judgement
    seat:
Oh, be swift, my soul, to answer Him! Be jubilant, my feet!
     Our God is marching on.

In the beauty of the lilies Christ was born across the sea,
With a glory in his bosom that transfigures you and me:
As he died to make men holy, let us die to make men free,
     While God is marching on.

Horatius

Thomas Babington Macaulay

1

Lars Porsena of Clusium
　By the Nine Gods he swore
That the great house of Tarquin
　Should suffer wrong no more.
By the Nine Gods he swore it,
　And named a trysting day,
And bade his messengers ride forth,
East and west and south and north,
　To summon his array.

2

East and west and south and north
　The messengers ride fast,
And tower and town and cottage
　Have heard the trumpet's blast.
Shame on the false Etruscan
　Who lingers in his home,
When Porsena of Clusium
　Is on the march for Rome.

3

The horsemen and the footmen
　　Are pouring in amain
From many a stately market-place;
　　From many a fruitful plain;
From many a lonely hamlet,
　　Which, hid by beech and pine,
Like an eagle's nest, hangs on the crest
　　Of purple Apennine;

4

From lordly Volaterræ,
　　Where scowls the far-famed hold
Piled by the hands of giants
　　For godlike kings of old;
From seagirt Populonia,
　　Whose sentinels descry
Sardinia's snowy mountain-tops
　　Fringing the southern sky;

5

From the proud mart of Pisæ,
　　Queen of the western waves,
Where ride Massilia's triremes
　　Heavy with fair-haired slaves;
From where sweet Clanis wanders
　　Through corn and vines and flowers;
From where Cortona lifts to heaven
　　Her diadem of towers.

6

Tall are the oaks whose acorns
    Drop in dark Auser's rill;
Fat are the stags that champ the boughs
    Of the Ciminian hill;
Beyond all streams Clitumnus
    Is to the herdsman dear;
Best of all pools the fowler loves
    The great Volsinian mere.

7

But now no stroke of woodman
    Is heard by Auser's rill;
No hunter tracks the stag's green path
    Up the Ciminian hill;
Unwatched along Clitumnus
    Grazes the milk-white steer;
Unharmed the water fowl may dip
    In the Volsinian mere.

8

The harvests of Arretium,
    This year, old men shall reap;
This year, young boys in Umbro
    Shall plunge the struggling sheep;
And in the vats of Luna,
    This year, the must shall foam
Round the white feet of laughing girls,
    Whose sires have marched to Rome.

9

There be thirty chosen prophets,
    The wisest of the land,
Who alway by Lars Porsena
    Both morn and evening stand:
Evening and morn the Thirty
    Have turned the verses o'er,
Traced from the right on linen white
    By mighty seers of yore.

10

And with one voice the Thirty
    Have their glad answer given:
"Go forth, go forth, Lars Porsena;
    Go forth, beloved of Heaven;
Go, and return in glory
    To Clusium's royal dome;
And hang round Nurscia's altars
    The golden shields of Rome."

11

And now hath every city
    Sent up her tale of men;
The foot are fourscore thousand,
    The horse are thousands ten.
Before the gates of Sutrium
    Is met the great array.
A proud man was Lars Porsena
    Upon the trysting day.

12

For all the Etruscan armies
　Were ranged beneath his eye,
And many a banished Roman,
　And many a stout ally;
And with a mighty following
　To join the muster came
The Tusculan Mamilius,
　Prince of the Latian name.

13

But by the yellow Tiber
　Was tumult and affright:
From all the spacious champaign
　To Rome men took their flight.
A mile around the city,
　The throng stopped up the ways;
A fearful sight it was to see
　Through two long nights and days.

14

For aged folk on crutches,
　And women great with child,
And mothers sobbing over babes
　That clung to them and smiled,
And sick men borne in litters
　High on the necks of slaves,
And troops of sun-burned husbandmen
　With reaping-hooks and staves.

And droves of mules and asses
   Laden with skins of wine,
And endless flocks of goats and sheep,
   And endless herds of kine,
And endless trains of waggons
   That creaked beneath the weight
Of corn-sacks and of household goods,
   Choked every roaring gate.

16

Now, from the rock Tarpeian,
   Could the wan burghers spy
The line of blazing villages
   Red in the midnight sky.
The Fathers of the City,
   They sat all night and day,
For every hour some horseman came
   With tidings of dismay.

17

To eastward and to westward
   Have spread the Tuscan bands;
Nor house, nor fence, nor dovecote
   In Crustumerium stands.
Verbenna down to Ostia
   Hath wasted all the plain;
Astur hath stormed Janiculum,
   And the stout guards are slain.

18

I wis, in all the Senate,
   There was no heart so bold,
But sore it ached, and fast it beat,
   When that ill news was told.
Forthwith up rose the Consul,
   Up rose the Fathers all;
In haste they girded up their gowns,
   And hied them to the wall.

19

They held a council standing
   Before the River-Gate;
Short time was there, ye well may guess,
   For musing or debate.
Out spake the Consul roundly:
   "The bridge must straight go down;
For, since Janiculum is lost,
   Nought else can save the town."

20

Just then a scout came flying,
   All wild with haste and fear:
"To arms! to arms! Sir Consul;
   Lars Porsena is here."
On the low hills to westward
   The Consul fixed his eye,
And saw the swarthy storm of dust
   Rise fast along the sky.

21

And nearer fast and nearer
   Doth the red whirlwind come;
And louder still and still more loud,
From underneath that rolling cloud,
Is heard the trumpet's war-note proud,
   The trampling, and the hum.
And plainly and more plainly
   Now through the gloom appears,
Far to left and far to right,
In broken gleams of dark-blue light,
The long array of helmets bright,
   The long array of spears.

22

And plainly and more plainly,
   Above that glimmering line,
Now might ye see the banners
   Of twelve fair cities shine;
But the banner of proud Clusium
   Was highest of them all,
The terror of the Umbrian,
   The terror of the Gaul.

23

And plainly and more plainly
   Now might the burghers know,
By port and vest, by horse and crest,
   Each warlike Lucumo.

There Cilnius of Arretium
    On his fleet roan was seen;
And Astur of the four-fold shield,
Girt with the brand none else may wield,
Tolumnius with the belt of gold,
And dark Verbenna from the hold
    By reedy Thrasymene.

24

Fast by the royal standard,
    O'erlooking all the war,
Lars Porsena of Clusium
    Sate in his ivory car.
By the right wheel rode Mamilius,
    Prince of the Latian name;
And by the left false Sextus,
    That wrought the deed of shame.

25

But when the face of Sextus
    Was seen among the foes,
A yell that rent the firmament
    From all the town arose.
On the house-tops was no woman
    But spat towards him and hissed;
No child but screamed out curses,
    And shook its little fist.

26

But the Consul's brow was sad,
    And the Consul's speech was low,
And darkly looked he at the wall,
    And darkly at the foe.
"Their van will be upon us
    Before the bridge goes down;
And if they once may win the bridge,
    What hope to save the town?"

27

Then out spake brave Horatius,
    The Captain of the gate:
"To every man upon this earth
    Death cometh soon or late.
And how can man die better
    Than facing fearful odds,
For the ashes of his fathers
    And the temples of his Gods,

28

"And for the tender mother
    Who dandled him to rest,
And for the wife who nurses
    His baby at her breast,
And for the holy maidens
    Who feed the eternal flame,
To save them from false Sextus
    That wrought the deed of shame?

29

"Hew down the bridge, Sir Consul,
    With all the speed ye may;
I, with two more to help me,
    Will hold the foe in play.
In yon strait path a thousand
    May well be stopped by three.
Now who will stand on either hand,
    And keep the bridge with me?"

30

Then out spake Spurius Lartius;
    A Ramnian proud was he:
"Lo, I will stand at thy right hand,
    And keep the bridge with thee."
And out spake strong Herminius;
    Of Titian blood was he:
"I will abide on thy left side,
    And keep the bridge with thee."

31

"Horatius," quoth the Consul,
    "As thou sayest, so let it be."
And straight against that great array
    Forth went the dauntless Three.
For Romans in Rome's quarrel
    Spared neither land nor gold,
Nor son nor wife, nor limb nor life,
    In the brave days of old.

32

Then none was for a party;
    Then all were for the state;
Then the great man helped the poor,
    And the poor man loved the great:
Then lands were fairly portioned;
    Then spoils were fairly sold:
The Romans were like brothers
    In the brave days of old.

33

Now Roman is to Roman
    More hateful than a foe,
And the Tribunes beard the high,
    And the Fathers grind the low.
As we wax hot in faction,
    In battle we wax cold:
Wherefore men fight not as they fought
    In the brave days of old.

34

Now while the Three were tightening
    Their harness on their backs,
The Consul was the foremost man
    To take in hand an axe:
And Fathers mixed with Commons
    Seized hatchet, bar, and crow,
And smote upon the planks above,
    And loosed the props below.

35

Meanwhile the Tuscan army,
    Right glorious to behold,
Came flashing back the noonday light,
Rank behind rank, like surges bright
    Of a broad sea of gold.
Four hundred trumpets sounded
    A peal of warlike glee,
As that great host, with measured tread,
And spears advanced, and ensigns spread,
Rolled slowly towards the bridge's head,
    Where stood the dauntless Three.

36

The Three stood calm and silent
    And looked upon the foes,
And a great shout of laughter
    From all the vanguard rose:
And forth three chiefs came spurring
    Before that deep array;
To earth they sprang, their swords they drew,
And lifted high their shields, and flew
    To win the narrow way;

37

Aunus from green Tifernum,
    Lord of the Hill of Vines;
And Seius, whose eight hundred slaves
    Sicken in Ilva's mines;

And Picus, long to Clusium
    Vassal in peace and war,
Who led to fight his Umbrian powers
From that gray crag where, girt with towers,
The fortress of Nequinum lowers
    O'er the pale waves of Nar.

38

Stout Lartius hurled down Aunus
    Into the stream beneath:
Herminius struck at Seius,
    And clove him to the teeth:
At Picus brave Horatius
    Darted one fiery thrust;
And the proud Umbrian's gilded arms
    Clashed in the bloody dust.

39

Then Ocnus of Falerii
    Rushed on the Roman Three;
And Lausulus of Urgo,
    The rover of the sea;
And Aruns of Volsinium,
    Who slew the great wild boar,
The great wild boar that had his den
Amidst the reeds of Cosa's fen,
And wasted fields, and slaughtered men,
    Along Albinia's shore.

40

Herminius smote down Aruns:
  Lartius laid Ocnus low:
Right to the heart of Lausulus
  Horatius sent a blow.
"Lie there," he cried, "fell pirate!
  No more, aghast and pale,
From Ostia's walls the crowd shall mark
The track of thy destroying bark.
No more Campania's hinds shall fly
To woods and caverns when they spy
  Thy thrice accursed sail."

41

But now no sound of laughter
  Was heard amongst the foes.
A wild and wrathful clamor
  From all the vanguard rose.
Six spears' lengths from the entrance
  Halted that deep array,
And for a space no man came forth
  To win the narrow way.

42

But hark! the cry is Astur:
  And lo! the ranks divide;
And the great Lord of Luna
  Comes with his stately stride.

Upon his ample shoulders
    Clangs loud the four-fold shield,
And in his hand he shakes the brand
    Which none but he can wield.

43

He smiled on those bold Romans
    A smile serene and high;
He eyed the flinching Tuscans,
    And scorn was in his eye.
Quoth he, "The she-wolf's litter
    Stand savagely at bay:
But will ye dare to follow,
    If Astur clears the way?"

44

Then, whirling up his broadsword
    With both hands to the height,
He rushed against Horatius,
    And smote with all his might.
With shield and blade Horatius
    Right deftly turned the blow.
The blow, though turned, came yet too nigh;
It missed his helm, but gashed his thigh:
The Tuscans raised a joyful cry
    To see the red blood flow.

45

He reeled, and on Herminius
    He leaned one breathing-space;
Then, like a wild cat mad with wounds,
    Sprang right at Astur's face.
Through teeth, and skull, and helmet,
    So fierce a thrust he sped,
The good sword stood a hand-breadth out
    Behind the Tuscan's head.

46

And the great Lord of Luna
    Fell at that deadly stroke,
As falls on Mount Alvernus
    A thunder-smitten oak.
Far o'er the crashing forest
    The giant arms lie spread;
And the pale augurs, muttering low,
    Gaze on the blasted head.

47

On Astur's throat Horatius
    Right firmly pressed his heel,
And thrice and four times tugged amain,
    Ere he wrenched out the steel.
"And see," he cried, "the welcome,
    Fair guests, that waits you here!
What noble Lucumo comes next
    To taste our Roman cheer?"

48

But at his haughty challenge
  A sullen murmur ran,
Mingled of wrath, and shame, and dread,
  Along that glittering van.
There lacked not men of prowess,
  Nor men of lordly race;
For all Etruria's noblest
  Were round the fatal place.

49

But all Etruria's noblest
  Felt their hearts sink to see
On the earth the bloody corpses,
  In the path the dauntless Three:
And, from the ghastly entrance
  Where those bold Romans stood,
All shrank, like boys who unaware,
Ranging the woods to start a hare,
Come to the mouth of the dark lair
Where, growling low, a fierce old bear
  Lies amidst bones and blood.

50

Was none who would be foremost
  To lead such dire attack;
But those behind cried "Forward!"
  And those before cried "Back!"
And backward now and forward
  Wavers the deep array;

And on the tossing sea of steel,
To and fro the standards reel;
And the victorious trumpet-peal
   Dies fitfully away.

51

Yet one man for one moment
   Strode out before the crowd;
Well known was he to all the Three,
   And they gave him greeting loud.
"Now welcome, welcome, Sextus!
   Now welcome to thy home!
Why dost thou stay, and turn away?
   Here lies the road to Rome."

52

Thrice looked he at the city;
   Thrice looked he at the dead;
And thrice came on in fury,
   And thrice turned back in dread:
And, white with fear and hatred,
   Scowled at the narrow way
Where, wallowing in a pool of blood,
   The bravest Tuscans lay.

53

But meanwhile axe and lever
   Have manfully been plied;
And now the bridge hangs tottering
   Above the boiling tide.

"Come back, come back, Horatius!"
  Loud cried the Fathers all.
"Back, Lartius! back, Herminius!
  Back, ere the ruin fall!"

54

Back darted Spurius Lartius;
  Herminius darted back:
And, as they passed, beneath their feet
  They felt the timbers crack.
But when they turned their faces,
  And on the farther shore
Saw brave Horatius stand alone,
  They would have crossed once more.

55

But with a crash like thunder
  Fell every loosened beam,
And, like a dam, the mighty wreck
  Lay right athwart the stream:
And a long shout of triumph
  Rose from the walls of Rome,
As to the highest turret-tops
  Was splashed the yellow foam.

56

And, like a horse unbroken
  When first he feels the rein,
The furious river struggled hard,
  And tossed his tawny mane;

And burst the curb, and bounded,
    Rejoicing to be free;
And whirling down, in fierce career,
Battlement, and plank, and pier,
    Rushed headlong to the sea.

57

Alone stood brave Horatius,
    But constant still in mind;
Thrice thirty thousand foes before,
    And the broad flood behind.
"Down with him!" cried false Sextus,
    With a smile on his pale face.
"Now yield thee," cried Lars Porsena,
    "Now yield thee to our grace."

58

Round turned he, as not deigning
    Those craven ranks to see;
Nought spake he to Lars Porsena,
    To Sextus nought spake he;
But he saw on Palatinus
    The white porch of his home;
And he spake to the noble river
    That rolls by the towers of Rome.

59

"Oh, Tiber! father Tiber!
    To whom the Romans pray,

A Roman's life, a Roman's arms,
    Take thou in charge this day!"
So he spake, and speaking sheathed
    The good sword by his side,
And with his harness on his back,
    Plunged headlong in the tide.

60

No sound of joy or sorrow
    Was heard from either bank;
But friends and foes in dumb surprise,
With parted lips and straining eyes,
    Stood gazing where he sank;
And when above the surges
    They saw his crest appear,
All Rome sent forth a rapturous cry,
And even the ranks of Tuscany
    Could scarce forbear to cheer.

61

But fiercely ran the current,
    Swollen high by months of rain:
And fast his blood was flowing;
    And he was sore in pain,
And heavy with his armor,
    And spent with changing blows:
And oft they thought him sinking,
    But still again he rose.

62

Never, I ween, did swimmer,
    In such an evil case,
Struggle through such a raging flood
    Safe to the landing place:
But his limbs were borne up bravely
    By the brave heart within,
And our good father Tiber
    Bare bravely up his chin.

63

"Curse on him!" quoth false Sextus;
    "Will not the villain drown?
But for this stay, ere close of day
    We should have sacked the town!"
"Heaven help him!" quoth Lars Porsena,
    "And bring him safe to shore;
For such a gallant feat of arms
    Was never seen before."

64

And now he feels the bottom;
    Now on dry earth he stands;
Now round him throng the Fathers
    To press his gory hands;
And now with shouts and clapping,
    And noise of weeping loud,
He enters through the River-Gate,
    Borne by the joyous crowd.

65

They gave him of the corn-land,
That was of public right,
As much as two strong oxen
Could plough from morn till night;
And they made a molten image,
And set it up on high,
And there it stands unto this day
To witness if I lie.

66

It stands in the Comitium,
Plain for all folk to see;
Horatius in his harness,
Halting upon one knee:
And underneath is written,
In letters all of gold,
How valiantly he kept the bridge
In the brave days of old.

67

And still his name sounds stirring
Unto the men of Rome,
As the trumpet-blast that cries to them
To charge the Volscian home;
And wives still pray to Juno
For boys with hearts as bold
As his who kept the bridge so well
In the brave days of old.

68

And in the nights of winter,
   When the cold north winds blow,
And the long howling of the wolves
   Is heard amidst the snow;
When round the lonely cottage
   Roars loud the tempest's din,
And the good logs of Algidus
   Roar louder yet within;

69

When the oldest cask is opened,
   And the largest lamp is lit,
When the chestnuts glow in the embers,
   And the kid turns on the spit;
When young and old in circle
   Around the firebrands close;
When the girls are weaving baskets,
   And the lads are shaping bows;

70

When the goodman mends his armor,
   And trims his helmet's plume;
When the goodwife's shuttle merrily
   Goes flashing through the loom;
With weeping and with laughter
   Still is the story told,
How well Horatius kept the bridge
   In the brave days of old.

The Charge of the Light Brigade

Alfred, Lord Tennyson

Half a league, half a league,
　　Half a league onward,
All in the valley of Death
　　Rode the six hundred.
"Forward, the Light Brigade!
Charge for the guns!" he said:
Into the valley of Death
　　Rode the six hundred.

"Forward, the Light Brigade!"
Was there a man dismay'd?
Not tho' the soldier knew
　　Some one had blunder'd:
Their's not to make reply,
Their's not to reason why,
Their's but to do and die:
Into the valley of Death
　　Rode the six hundred.

Cannon to right of them,
Cannon to left of them,
Cannon in front of them
　　Volley'd and thunder'd;

Storm'd at with shot and shell,
Boldly they rode and well,
Into the jaws of Death,
Into the mouth of Hell
   Rode the six hundred.

Flash'd all their sabres bare,
Flash'd as they turn'd in air
Sabring the gunners there,
Charging an army, while
   All the world wonder'd:
Plunged in the battery-smoke
Right thro' the line they broke;
Cossack and Russian
Reel'd from the sabre-stroke
   Shatter'd and sunder'd.
Then they rode back, but not
   Not the six hundred.

Cannon to right of them,
Cannon to left of them,
Cannon behind them
   Volley'd and thunder'd;
Storm'd at with shot and shell,
While horse and hero fell,
They that had fought so well
Came thro' the jaws of Death,
Back from the mouth of Hell,
All that was left of them,
   Left of six hundred.

When can their glory fade?
O the wild charge they made!
　　All the world wonder'd.
Honor the charge they made!
Honor the Light Brigade,
　　Noble six hundred!

The Battle of Blenheim

Robert Southey

1

It was a summer evening,
   Old Kaspar's work was done,
And he before his cottage door
   Was sitting in the sun,
And by him sported on the green
His little grandchild Wilhelmine.

2

She saw her brother Peterkin
   Roll something large and round,
Which he beside the rivulet
   In playing there had found;
He came to ask what he had found,
That was so large, and smooth, and round.

3

Old Kaspar took it from the boy,
   Who stood expectant by;
And then the old man shook his head,
   And, with a natural sigh,
"'Tis some poor fellow's skull," said he,
"Who fell in the great victory.

4

"I find them in the garden,
    For there's many here about;
And often when I go to plough,
    The ploughshare turns them out!
For many thousand men," said he,
"Were slain in that great victory."

5

"Now tell us what 'twas all about,"
    Young Peterkin, he cries;
And little Wilhelmine looks up
    With wonder-waiting eyes;
"Now tell us all about the war,
And what they fought each other for."

6

"It was the English," Kaspar cried,
    "Who put the French to rout;
But what they fought each other for,
    I could not well make out;
But everybody said," quoth he,
"That 'twas a famous victory.

7

"My father lived at Blenheim then,
    Yon little stream hard by;
They burnt his dwelling to the ground,
    And he was forced to fly;
So with his wife and child he fled,
Nor had he where to rest his head.

8

"With fire and sword the country round
    Was wasted far and wide,
And many a childing mother then,
    And new-born baby died;
But things like that, you know, must be
At every famous victory.

9

"They say it was a shocking sight
    After the field was won;
For many thousand bodies here
    Lay rotting in the sun;
But things like that, you know, must be
After a famous victory.

10

"Great praise the Duke of Marlbro' won,
    And our good Prince Eugene."
"Why 'twas a very wicked thing!"
    Said little Wilhelmine.
"Nay...nay...my little girl," quoth he,
"It was a famous victory.

11

"And everybody praised the Duke
    Who this great fight did win."
"But what good came of it at last?"
    Quoth little Peterkin.
"Why that I cannot tell," said he
"But 'twas a famous victory."

For Want of a Nail

Anonymous

For want of a nail the shoe was lost,
For want of a shoe the horse was lost,
For want of a horse the rider was lost,
For want of a rider the battle was lost,
For want of a battle the kingdom was lost,
And all for the want of a horseshoe nail.

The Song of the Bow

Sir Arthur Conan Doyle

What of the bow?
  The bow was made in England:
Of true wood, of yew wood,
  The wood of English bows;
    So men who are free
    Love the old yew-tree
And the land where the yew-tree grows.

What of the cord?
  The cord was made in England:
A rough cord, a tough cord,
  A cord that bowmen love;
    And so we will sing
    Of the hempen string
And the land where the cord was wove.

What of the shaft?
  The shaft was cut in England:
A long shaft, a strong shaft,
  Barbed and trim and true;
    So we'll drink all together
    To the gray goose feather
And the land where the gray goose flew.

What of the mark?
    Ah, seek it not in England:
A bold mark, our old mark
    Is waiting over-sea
        When the strings harp in chorus
        And the lion flag is o'er us
It is there that our mark shall be.

What of the men?
    The men were bred in England:
The bowmen—the yeomen—
    The lads of dale and fell.
        Here's to you—and to you!
        To the hearts that are true
And the land where the true hearts dwell.

Drake's Drum

Sir Henry Newbolt

Drake he's in his hammock an' a thousand mile away,
   (Capten, art tha sleepin' there below?)
Slung atween the round shot in Nombre Dios Bay,
   An' dreamin' arl the time o' Plymouth Hoe.
Yarnder lumes the Island, yarnder lie the ships,
   Wi' sailor lads a-dancin' heel-an'-toe,
An' the shore-lights flashin', an' the night-tide dashin',
   He sees et arl so plainly as he saw et long ago.

Drake he was a Devon man, an' ruled the Devon seas,
   (Capten, art tha sleepin' there below?),
Rovin' tho' his death fell, he went wi' heart at ease,
   An' dreamin' arl the time o' Plymouth Hoe.
"Take my drum to England, hang et by the shore,
   Strike et when your powder's runnin' low;
If the Dons sight Devon, I'll quit the port o' Heaven,
   An' drum them up the Channel as we drumm'd them
     long ago."

Drake he's in his hammock till the great Armadas come,
   (Capten, art tha sleepin' there below?),
Slung atween the round shot, listenin' for the drum,
   An' dreamin' arl the time o' Plymouth Hoe.

Call him on the deep sea, call him up the Sound,
  Call him when ye sail to meet the foe;
Where the old trade's plyin' an' the old flag flyin'
  They shall find him ware an' wakin', as they found him
    long ago!

Gunga Din

Rudyard Kipling

You may talk o' gin and beer
When you're quartered safe out 'ere,
An' you're sent to penny-fights an' Aldershot it;
But when it comes to slaughter
You will do your work on water,
An' you'll lick the bloomin' boots of
   'im that's got it.
Now in Injia's sunny clime,
Where I used to spend my time
A-servin' of 'Er Majesty the Queen,
Of all them blackfaced crew
The finest man I knew
Was our regimental bhisti, Gunga Din.
        He was "Din! Din! Din!
   "You limpin' lump o' brick-dust, Gunga Din!
      "Hi! slippery *kitherao*!
      "Water, get it! *Panee lao*!
   "You squidgy-nosed old idol, Gunga Din."

The uniform 'e wore
Was nothin' much before,
An' rather less than 'arf o' that be'ind,
For a piece o' twisty rag
An' a goatskin water-bag
Was all the field-equipment 'e could find.

When the sweatin' troop-train lay
In a sidin' through the day,
Where the 'eat would make your bloomin' eyebrows crawl,
We shouted "Harry By!"
Till our throats were bricky-dry,
Then we wopped 'im 'cause 'e couldn't serve us all.
       It was "Din! Din! Din!
   "You 'eathen, where the mischief 'ave you been?
       "You put some *juldee* in it
       "Or I'll *marrow* you this minute
       "If you don't fill up my helmet, Gunga Din!"

'E would dot an' carry one
Till the longest day was done;
An' 'e didn't seem to know the use o' fear.
If we charged or broke or cut,
You could bet your bloomin' nut,
'E'd be waitin' fifty paces right flank rear.
With 'is mussick on 'is back,
'E would skip with our attack,
An' watch us till the bugles made "Retire,"
An' for all 'is dirty 'ide
'E was white, clear white, inside
When 'e went to tend the wounded under fire!
       It was "Din! Din! Din!"
  With the bullets kickin' dust-spots on the green.
       When the cartridges ran out,
       You could hear the front-files shout,
  "Hi! ammunition-mules an' Gunga Din!"

I sha'n't forgit the night
When I dropped be'ind the fight
With a bullet where my belt-plate should 'a' been.
I was chokin' mad with thirst,
An' the man that spied me first
Was our good old grinnin', gruntin' Gunga Din.
'E lifted up my 'ead,
An' he plugged me where I bled,
An' 'e guv me 'arf-a-pint o' water-green:
It was crawlin' and it stunk,
But of all the drinks I've drunk,
I'm gratefullest to one from Gunga Din.
       It was "Din! Din! Din!
  "'Ere's a beggar with a bullet through 'is spleen;
      "'E's chawin' up the ground,
     "An' 'e's kickin' all around:
  "For Gawd's sake git the water, Gunga Din!"

'E carried me away
To where a dooli lay,
An' a bullet come an' drilled the beggar clean.
'E put me safe inside,
An' just before 'e died,
"I 'ope you liked your drink," sez Gunga Din.
So I'll meet 'im later on
At the place where 'e is gone—
Where it's always double drill and no canteen;
'E'll be squattin' on the coals
Givin' drink to poor damned souls,

An' I'll get a swig in hell from Gunga Din!
    Yes, Din! Din! Din!
  You Lazarushian-leather Gunga Din!
        Though I've belted you and flayed you,
        By the livin' Gawd that made you,
  You're a better man than I am, Gunga Din!

THINGS TO THINK ABOUT

The ways of the world, and the lives of the people and things in it, are not always easy to understand. Sometimes logic and reason fail us, and we have to rely on some kind of spiritual understanding of the way things are. Something about a great poem gets to the heart of things without necessarily spelling out its meaning. When you read a poem like that, you sometimes feel that a window has opened on the universe, giving you a glimpse of something you have never seen before, something that is undeniably true, which will stay with you in some form for the rest of your life. Perhaps the poems in this section will help you see some parts of the world and your place in it a little more clearly.

Ozymandias

Percy Bysshe Shelley

I met a traveler from an antique land
Who said: Two vast and trunkless legs of stone
Stand in the desert... Near them, on the sand,
Half sunk, a shattered visage lies, whose frown,
And wrinkled lip, and sneer of cold command,
Tell that its sculptor well those passions read
Which yet survive, stamped on these lifeless things,
The hand that mocked them, and the heart that fed:
And on the pedestal these words appear:
"My name is Ozymandias, king of kings:
Look on my works, ye Mighty, and despair!"
Nothing beside remains. Round the decay
Of that colossal wreck, boundless and bare
The lone and level sands stretch far away.

Sea Fever

John Masefield

I must go down to the seas again, to the lonely sea and
the sky,
And all I ask is a tall ship and a star to steer her by;
And the wheel's kick and the wind's song and the white
sail's shaking,
And a gray mist on the sea's face, and a gray dawn
breaking.

I must go down to the seas again, for the call of the running
tide
Is a wild call and a clear call that may not be denied;
And all I ask is a windy day with the white clouds flying,
And the flung spray and the blown spume, and the sea-
gulls crying.

I must go down to the seas again, to the vagrant gypsy life,
To the gull's way and the whale's way where the wind's like
a whetted knife;
And all I ask is a merry yarn from a laughing fellow-rover,
And quiet sleep and a sweet dream when the long trick's
over.

To See

William Blake

To see a world in a grain of sand
  And a Heaven in a wild flower,
Hold Infinity in the palm of your hand
  And Eternity in an hour.

And Did Those Feet

William Blake

And did those feet in ancient time
Walk upon England's mountains green?
And was the holy Lamb of God
On England's pleasant pastures seen?

And did the Countenance Divine
Shine forth upon our clouded hills?
And was Jerusalem builded here,
Among these dark Satanic Mills?

Bring me my Bow of burning gold:
Bring me my Arrows of desire:
Bring me my Spear: O clouds unfold!
Bring me my Chariot of fire!

I will not cease from Mental Fight,
Nor shall my Sword sleep in my hand,
Till we have built Jerusalem
In England's green & pleasant Land.

All Things Bright and Beautiful

Cecil Frances Alexander

All things bright and beautiful,
　　All creatures great and small,
All things wise and wonderful,
　　The Lord God made them all.

Each little flower that opens,
　　Each little bird that sings,
He made their glowing colors,
　　He made their tiny wings.

The rich man in his castle,
　　The poor man at his gate,
God made them, high or lowly,
　　And ordered their estate.

The purple-headed mountain,
　　The river running by,
The sunset, and the morning,
　　That brightens up the sky,

The cold wind in the winter,
　　The pleasant summer sun,
The ripe fruits in the garden,
　　He made them every one.

The tall trees in the greenwood,
    The meadows where we play,
The rushes by the water,
    We gather every day;—

He gave us eyes to see them,
    And lips that we might tell,
How great is God Almighty,
    Who has made all things well.

Richard Cory

Edwin Arlington Robinson

Whenever Richard Cory went down town,
We people on the pavement looked at him:
He was a gentleman from sole to crown,
Clean favored, and imperially slim.

And he was always quietly arrayed,
And he was always human when he talked;
But still he fluttered pulses when he said,
"Good-morning," and he glittered when he walked.

And he was rich—yes, richer than a king—
And admirably schooled in every grace:
In fine, we thought that he was everything
To make us wish that we were in his place.

So on we worked, and waited for the light,
And went without the meat, and cursed the bread;
And Richard Cory, one calm summer night,
Went home and put a bullet through his head.

The Road Not Taken

Robert Frost

Two roads diverged in a yellow wood,
And sorry I could not travel both
And be one traveler, long I stood
And looked down one as far as I could
To where it bent in the undergrowth;

Then took the other, as just as fair,
And having perhaps the better claim,
Because it was grassy and wanted wear;
Though as for that the passing there
Had worn them really about the same,

And both that morning equally lay
In leaves no step had trodden black.
Oh, I kept the first for another day!
Yet knowing how way leads on to way,
I doubted if I should ever come back.

I shall be telling this with a sigh
Somewhere ages and ages hence:
Two roads diverged in a wood, and I—
I took the one less traveled by,
And that has made all the difference.

Stopping by Woods on a Snowy Evening

Robert Frost

Whose woods these are I think I know.
His house is in the village though;
He will not see me stopping here
To watch his woods fill up with snow.

My little horse must think it queer
To stop without a farmhouse near
Between the woods and frozen lake
The darkest evening of the year.

He gives his harness bells a shake
To ask if there is some mistake.
The only other sound's the sweep
Of easy wind and downy flake.

The woods are lovely, dark and deep,
But I have promises to keep,
And miles to go before I sleep,
And miles to go before I sleep.

Fog

Carl Sandburg

The fog comes
on little cat feet.

It sits looking
over harbor and city
on silent haunches
and then moves on.

Spring and Fall

Gerard Manley Hopkins
To a Young Child

Margaret, are you grieving
Over Goldengrove unleaving?
Leaves, like the things of man, you
With your fresh thoughts care for, can you?
Ah! as the heart grows older
It will come to such sights colder
By and by, nor spare a sigh
Though worlds of wanwood leafmeal lie;
And yet you *will* weep and know why.
Now no matter, child, the name:
Sorrow's springs are the same.
Nor mouth had, no nor mind, expressed
What heart heard of, ghost guessed:
It is the blight man was born for,
It is Margaret you mourn for.

Invictus

William Ernest Henley

Out of the night that covers me,
　Black as the pit from pole to pole,
I thank whatever gods may be
　For my unconquerable soul.

In the fell clutch of circumstance
　I have not winced nor cried aloud:
Under the bludgeonings of chance
　My head is bloody, but unbow'd.

Beyond this place of wrath and tears
　Looms but the Horror of the shade,
And yet the menace of the years
　Finds and shall find me unafraid.

It matters not how strait the gate,
　How charged with punishments the scroll,
I am the master of my fate:
　I am the captain of my soul.

From The Lay of the Last Minstrel

Sir Walter Scott

Breathes there the man with soul so dead,
Who never to himself hath said,
    This is my own, my native land!
Whose heart hath ne'er within him burn'd,
As home his footsteps he hath turn'd
    From wandering on a foreign strand!
If such there breathe, go, mark him well;
For him no Minstrel raptures swell;
High though his titles, proud his name,
Boundless his wealth as wish can claim;
Despite those titles, power, and pelf,
The wretch, concentred all in self,
Living, shall forfeit fair renown,
And, doubly dying, shall go down
To the vile dust, from whence he sprung,
Unwept, unhonor'd, and unsung

The New Colossus

Emma Lazarus

Not like the brazen giant of Greek fame,
With conquering limbs astride from land to land;
Here at our sea-washed, sunset gates shall stand
A mighty woman with a torch, whose flame
Is the imprisoned lightning, and her name
Mother of Exiles. From her beacon-hand
Glows world-wide welcome; her mild eyes command
The air-bridged harbor that twin cities frame.
"Keep, ancient lands, your storied pomp!" cries she
With silent lips. "Give me your tired, your poor,
Your huddled masses yearning to breathe free,
The wretched refuse of your teeming shore.
Send these, the homeless, tempest-tost to me,
I lift my lamp beside the golden door!"

If—

Rudyard Kipling

If you can keep your head when all about you
    Are losing theirs and blaming it on you;
If you can trust yourself when all men doubt you,
    But make allowance for their doubting too;
If you can wait and not be tired by waiting,
    Or being lied about, don't deal in lies,
Or being hated, don't give way to hating,
    And yet don't look too good, nor walk too wise:

If you can dream—and not make dreams your master;
    If you can think—and not make thought your aim;
If you can meet with Triumph and Disaster
    And treat those two impostors just the same;
If you can bear to hear the truth you've spoken
    Twisted by knaves to make a trap for fools,
Or watch the things you gave your life to, broken,
    And stoop and build 'em up with worn-out tools:

If you can make one heap of all your winnings
    And risk it on one turn of pitch-and-toss,
And lose, and start again at your beginnings
    And never breathe a word about your loss;

If you can force your heart and nerve and sinew
    To serve your turn long after they are gone,
And so hold on when there is nothing in you
    Except the Will which says to them: "Hold on!"

If you can talk with crowds and keep your virtue,
    Or walk with Kings—nor lose the common touch,
If neither foes nor loving friends can hurt you,
    If all men count with you, but none too much;
If you can fill the unforgiving minute
    With sixty seconds' worth of distance run,
Yours is the Earth and everything that's in it,
    And—which is more—you'll be a Man, my son!

The Thousandth Man

Rudyard Kipling

One man in a thousand, Solomon says,
    Will stick more close than a brother.
And it's worth while seeking him half your days
    If you find him before the other.
Nine hundred and ninety-nine depend
    On what the world sees in you,
But the Thousandth Man will stand your friend
    With the whole round world agin you.

'Tis neither promise nor prayer nor show
    Will settle the finding for 'ee.
Nine hundred and ninety-nine of 'em go
    By your looks or your acts or your glory.
But if he finds you and you find him,
    The rest of the world don't matter;
For the Thousandth Man will sink or swim
    With you in any water.

You can use his purse with no more talk
    Than he uses yours for his spendings;
And laugh and meet in your daily walk
    As though there had been no lendings.

Nine hundred and ninety-nine of 'em call
    For silver and gold in their dealings;
But the Thousandth Man he's worth 'em all,
    Because you can show him your feelings!

His wrong's your wrong, and his right's your right,
    In season or out of season.
Stand up and back it in all men's sight—
    With *that* for your only reason!
Nine hundred and ninety-nine can't bide
    The shame or mocking or laughter,
But the Thousandth Man will stand by your side
    To the gallows-foot—and after!

Sonnet 29

William Shakespeare

When, in disgrace with Fortune and men's eyes,
I all alone beweep my outcast state,
And trouble deaf heaven with my bootless cries,
And look upon myself and curse my fate,
Wishing me like to one more rich in hope,
Featured like him, like him with friends possessed,
Desiring this man's art, and that man's scope,
With what I most enjoy contented least;
Yet in these thoughts myself almost despising,
Haply I think on thee, and then my state,
Like to the lark at break of day arising
From sullen earth, sings hymns at heaven's gate;
  For thy sweet love rememb'red such wealth brings
  That then I scorn to change my state with kings.

Loveliest of Trees, the Cherry Now

A. E. Housman

Loveliest of trees, the cherry now
Is hung with bloom along the bough,
And stands about the woodland ride
Wearing white for Eastertide.

Now, of my threescore years and ten,
Twenty will not come again,
And take from seventy springs a score,
It only leaves me fifty more.

And since to look at things in bloom
Fifty springs are little room,
About the woodlands I will go
To see the cherry hung with snow.

TONGUE
TWISTERS

None of these little verses look very hard to say when you're reading them to yourself, but try saying them out loud and fast! It's even more fun when you read them with a friend, to see whose tongue twists most (or least!).

Peter Piper picked a peck of pickled pepper;
A peck of pickled pepper Peter Piper picked;
If Peter Piper picked a peck of pickled pepper,
Where's the peck of pickled pepper Peter Piper picked?

Betty Botter bought some butter,
But, she said, the butter's bitter;
If I put it in my batter
It will make my batter bitter,
But a bit of better butter
Will make my batter better.
So she bought a bit of butter
Better than her bitter butter,
And she put it in her batter
And the batter was not bitter.
So t'was better Betty Botter bought a bit of better butter.

A flea and a fly flew up in a flue.
Said the flea, "Let us fly!"
Said the fly, "Let us flee!"
So they flew through a flaw in the flue.

A tutor who tooted the flute
Tried to tutor two tooters to toot.
    Said the two to the tutor,
    "Is it harder to toot or
To tutor two tooters to toot?"

How much wood could a woodchuck chuck
If a woodchuck could chuck wood?
As much wood as a woodchuck would,
If a woodchuck could chuck wood.

LIMERICKS

Limerick is a town in Ireland, but that doesn't really seem to have much if anything to do with the poems called by that name! These short, humorous verses were made popular in the nineteenth century by the poet Edward Lear (some of his longer nonsense poems are also included in this book), but they are so simple that with a little thought anyone can write one. Reading them is like eating peanuts and popcorn—it's hard to stop!

There Was an Old Man with a Beard

Edward Lear

There was an Old Man with a beard,
Who said, "It is just as I feared!—
Two Owls and a Hen, four Larks and a Wren.
Have all built their nests in my beard."

There Was a Young Lady of Portugal

Edward Lear

There was a Young Lady of Portugal,
Whose ideas were excessively nautical;
She climbed up a tree to examine the sea,
But declared she would never leave Portugal.

There Was a Young Lady Whose Chin

Edward Lear

There was a Young Lady whose chin,
Resembled the point of a pin;
So she had it made sharp, and purchased a harp,
And played several tunes with her chin.

There Was an Old Man
in a Boat

Edward Lear

There was an Old Man in a boat,
Who said, "I'm afloat! I'm afloat!"
When they said, "No! you ain't!" he was ready to faint,
That unhappy Old Man in a boat.

There Once Was a Man from Nantucket

Anonymous

There once was a man from Nantucket,
Who kept all his cash in a bucket.
    But his daughter, named Nan,
    Ran away with a man,
And as for the bucket, Nantucket.

There Once Was a Person from Lyme

Anonymous

There once was a person from Lyme
Who married three wives at a time.
>When asked, "Why a third?"
>He replied, "One's absurd,
And bigamy, sir, is a crime!"

JUST FOR LAUGHS

The poems in this section are long and short, old and new, but they all have one thing in common—they were written to amuse their readers (and probably the poets who wrote them as well). Some of these poems, like the ones by Edward Lear and Lewis Carroll, the author of Alice in Wonderland, *are complete and wonderful nonsense from beginning to end. Others, like Ernest Thayer's "Casey at the Bat" or Shel Silverstein's "A Boy Named Sue," start out as though they have something serious to say, but they soon turn hilariously silly. Whatever your mood, reading a few of these poems is sure to improve it!*

The Deacon's Masterpiece

OR, THE WONDERFUL "ONE-HOSS SHAY"

A LOGICAL STORY

Oliver Wendell Holmes

Have you heard of the wonderful one-hoss shay,
That was built in such a logical way
It ran a hundred years to a day,
And then, of a sudden, it—ah, but stay,
I'll tell you what happened without delay,
Scaring the parson into fits,
Frightening people out of their wits,—
Have you ever heard of that, I say?

Seventeen hundred and fifty-five.
Georgius Secundus was then alive,—
Snuffy old drone from the German hive.
That was the year when Lisbon-town
Saw the earth open and gulp her down,
And Braddock's army was done so brown,
Left without a scalp to its crown.
It was on the terrible Earthquake-day
That the Deacon finished the one-hoss shay.

Now in building of chaises, I tell you what,
There is always *somewhere* a weakest spot,—
In hub, tire, felloe, in spring or thill,
In panel, or crossbar, or floor, or still,

In screw, bolt, thoroughbrace,—lurking still,
Find it somewhere you must and will,—
Above or below, or within or without,—
And that's the reason, beyond a doubt,
That a chaise *breaks down*, but does n't *wear out*.

But the Deacon swore (as Deacons do,
With an "I dew vum," or an "I tell *yeou*")
He would build one shay to beat the taown
N' the keounty 'n' all the kentry raoun';
It should be so built that it *could n'* break daown;
"Fur," said the Deacon, "'t's mighty plain
Thut the weakes' place mus' stan' the strain;
'N' the way t' fix it, uz I maintain, is only jest
T' make that place uz strong uz the rest."

So the Deacon inquired of the village folk
Where he could find the strongest oak,
That could n't be split nor bent nor broke,—
That was for spokes and floor and sills;
He sent for lancewood to make the thills;
The crossbars were ash, from the straightest trees,
The panels of white-wood, that cuts like cheese,
But lasts like iron for things like these;
The hubs of logs from the "Settler's ellum,"—
Last of its timber,—they could n't sell 'em,
Never an axe had seen their chips,
And the wedges flew from between their lips,
Their blunt ends frizzled like celery-tips;

Step and prop-iron, bolt and screw,
Spring, tire, axle, and linchpin too,
Steel of the finest, bright and blue;
Thoroughbrace bison-skin, thick and wide;
Boot, top, dasher, from tough old hide
Found in the pit when the tanner died.
That was the way he "put her through."
"There!" said the Deacon, "naow she'll dew!"

Do! I tell you, I rather guess
She was a wonder, and nothing less!
Colts grew horses, beards turned gray,
Deacon and deaconess dropped away,
Children and grandchildren—where were they?
But there stood the stout old one-hoss shay
As fresh as on Lisbon-earthquake day!

Eighteen hundred;—It came and found
The Deacon's masterpiece strong and sound.
Eighteen hundred increased by ten;—
"Hahnsum kerridge" they called it then.
Eighteen hundred and twenty came;—
Running as usual; much the same.
Thirty and forty at last arrive,
And then come fifty, and FIFTY-FIVE.

Little of all we value here
Wakes on the morn of its hundredth year
Without both feeling and looking queer.
In fact, there's nothing that keeps its youth,
So far as I know, but a tree and truth.
(This is a moral that runs at large;
Take it.—You're welcome.—No extra charge.)

First of november.—the Earthquake day,—
There are traces of age in the one-hoss shay,
A general flavor of mild decay,
But nothing local, as one may say.
There could n't be,—for the Deacon's art
Had made it so like in every part
That there wasn't a chance for one to start.
For the wheels were just as strong as the thills,
And the floor was just as strong as the sills,
And the panels just as strong as the floor,
And the whipple-tree neither less nor more,
And the back crossbar as strong as the fore,
And spring and axle and hub *encore*,
And yet, *as a whole*, it is past a doubt
In another hour it will be *worn out!*

First of November, 'Fifty-five!
This morning the parson takes a drive.
Now, small boys, get out of the way!
Here comes the wonderful one-hoss shay,
Drawn by a rat-tailed, ewe-necked bay.
"Huddup!" said the parson.—Off went they.

The parson was working his Sunday's text,—
Had got to *fifthly,* and stopped perplexed
At what the—Moses—was coming next.
All at once the horse stood still.
Close by the meet'n'-house on the hill.
First a shiver, and then a thrill,
Then something decidedly like a spill,—
And the parson was sitting upon a rock,
At half past nine by the meet'n'-house clock,—
Just the hour of the Earthquake shock!
What do you think the parson found,
When he got up and stared around?
The poor old chaise in a heap or mound,
As if it had been to the mill and ground!
You see, of course, if you're not a dunce,
How it went to pieces all at once,—
All at once, and nothing first,—
Just as bubbles do when they burst.

End of the wonderful one-hoss shay.
Logic is logic. That's all I say.

The Height of the Ridiculous

Oliver Wendell Holmes

I wrote some lines once on a time
    In wondrous merry mood,
And thought, as usual, men would say
    They were exceeding good.

They were so queer, so very queer,
    I laughed as I would die;
Albeit, in the general way,
    A sober man am I.

I called my servant, and he came;
    How kind it was of him
To mind a slender man like me,
    He of the mighty limb!

"These to the printer," I exclaimed,
    And, in my humorous way,
I added, (as a trifling jest,)
    "There'll be the devil to pay."

He took the paper, and I watched,
    And saw him peep within;
At the first line he read, his face
    Was all upon the grin.

He read the next; the grin grew broad,
    And shot from ear to ear;
He read the third; a chuckling noise
    I now began to hear.

The fourth; he broke into a roar;
    The fifth; his waistband split;
The sixth; he burst five buttons off,
    And tumbled in a fit.

Ten days and nights, with sleepless eye,
    I watched that wretched man,
And since, I never dare to write
    As funny as I can.

Jabberwocky

Lewis Carroll

'Twas brillig, and the slithy toves
   Did gyre and gimble in the wabe;
All mimsy were the borogoves,
      And the mome raths outgrabe

"Beware the Jabberwock, my son!
   The jaws that bite, the claws that catch!
Beware the Jubjub bird, and shun
      The frumious Bandersnatch!"

He took his vorpal sword in hand:
   Long time the manxome foe he sought—
So rested he by the Tumtum tree,
      And stood awhile in thought.

And as in uffish thought he stood,
   The Jabberwock, with eyes of flame,
Came whiffling through the tulgey wood,
      And burbled as it came!

One, two! One, two! And through and through
   The vorpal blade went snicker-snack!
He left it dead, and with its head
      He went galumphing back.

The Walrus and the Carpenter

Lewis Carroll

The sun was shining on the sea,
   Shining with all his might:
He did his very best to make
   The billows smooth and bright—
And this was odd, because it was
   The middle of the night.

The moon was shining sulkily,
   Because she thought the sun
Had got no business to be there
   After the day was done—
"It's very rude of him," she said,
   "To come and spoil the fun!"

The sea was wet as wet could be,
   The sands were dry as dry.
You could not see a cloud, because
   No cloud was in the sky:
No birds were flying overhead—
   There were no birds to fly.

The Walrus and the Carpenter
　　Were walking close at hand;
They wept like anything to see
　　Such quantities of sand:
"If this were only cleared away,"
　　They said, "it *would* be grand!"

"If seven maids with seven mops
　　Swept it for half a year,
Do you suppose," the Walrus said,
　　"That they could get it clear?"
"I doubt it," said the Carpenter,
　　And shed a bitter tear.

"O Oysters, come and walk with us!"
　　The Walrus did beseech.
"A pleasant walk, a pleasant talk,
　　Along the briny beach:
We cannot do with more than four,
　　To give a hand to each."

The eldest Oyster looked at him,
　　But never a word he said:
The eldest Oyster winked his eye,
　　And shook his heavy head—
Meaning to say he did not choose
　　To leave the oyster-bed.

But four young Oysters hurried up,
    All eager for the treat:
Their coats were brushed, their faces washed,
    Their shoes were clean and neat—
And this was odd, because, you know,
    They hadn't any feet.

Four other Oysters followed them,
    And yet another four;
And thick and fast they came at last,
    And more, and more, and more—
All hopping through the frothy waves,
    And scrambling to the shore.

The Walrus and the Carpenter
    Walked on a mile or so,
And then they rested on a rock
    Conveniently low:
And all the little Oysters stood
    And waited in a row.

"The time has come," the Walrus said,
    "To talk of many things:
Of shoes—and ships—and sealing-wax—
    Of cabbages—and kings—
And why the sea is boiling hot—
    And whether pigs have wings."

"But wait a bit," the Oysters cried,
    "Before we have our chat;
For some of us are out of breath,
    And all of us are fat!"
"No hurry!" said the Carpenter.
    They thanked him much for that.

"A loaf of bread," the Walrus said,
    "Is what we chiefly need:
Pepper and vinegar besides
    Are very good indeed—
Now if you're ready, Oysters dear,
    We can begin to feed."

"But not on us!" the Oysters cried,
    Turning a little blue.
"After such kindness, that would be
    A dismal thing to do!"
"The night is fine," the Walrus said.
    "Do you admire the view?

"It was so kind of you to come!
    And you are very nice!"
The Carpenter said nothing but
    "Cut us another slice:
I wish you were not quite so deaf—
    I've had to ask you twice!"

"It seems a shame," the Walrus said,
  "To play them such a trick,
After we've brought them out so far,
  And made them trot so quick!"
The Carpenter said nothing but
  "The butter's spread too thick!"

"I weep for you," the Walrus said:
  "I deeply sympathize."
With sobs and tears he sorted out
  Those of the largest size,
Holding his pocket-handkerchief
  Before his streaming eyes.

"O Oysters," said the Carpenter,
  "You've had a pleasant run!
Shall we be trotting home again?"
  But answer came there none—
And this was scarcely odd, because
  They'd eaten every one.

Beautiful Soup

Lewis Carroll

Beautiful Soup, so rich and green,
Waiting in a hot tureen!
Who for such dainties would not stoop!
Soup of the evening, beautiful Soup!
Soup of the evening, beautiful Soup!
  Beau—ootiful Soo—oop!
  Beau—ootiful Soo—oop!
Soo—oop of the e—e—evening,
  Beautiful, beautiful Soup!

Beautiful Soup! Who cares for fish,
Game, or any other dish?
Who would not give all else for two p
ennyworth only of beautiful Soup?
Pennyworth only of beautiful Soup?
  Beau—ootiful Soo—oop!
  Beau—ootiful Soo—oop!
Soo—oop of the e—e—evening,
  Beautiful, beauti—FUL SOUP!

George

WHO PLAYED WITH A DANGEROUS TOY,
AND SUFFERED A CATASTROPHE
OF CONSIDERABLE DIMENSIONS.

Hilaire Belloc

When George's Grandmamma was told
That George had been as good as Gold,
She Promised in the Afternoon
To buy him an *Immense BALLOON*.
And so she did; but when it came,
It got into the candle flame,
And being of a dangerous sort
Exploded with a loud report!
The Lights went out! The Windows broke!
The Room was filled with reeking smoke.
And in the darkness shrieks and yells
Were mingled with Electric Bells,
And falling masonry and groans,
And crunching, as of broken bones,
And dreadful shrieks, when, worst of all,
The House itself began to fall!
It tottered, shuddering to and fro,
Then crashed into the street below—
Which happened to be Savile Row.

When Help arrived, among the Dead
Were Cousin Mary, Little Fred,
The Footmen (both of them), The Groom,
The man that cleaned the Billiard-Room,
The Chaplain, and The Still-Room Maid.
And I am dreadfully afraid
That Monsieur Champignon, the Chef,
Will now be permanently deaf—
And both his Aides are much the same;
While George, who was in part to blame,
Received, you will regret to hear,
A nasty lump behind the ear.

Moral

The moral is that little Boys
Should not be given dangerous Toys.

Eletelephony

Laura Richards

Once there was an elephant,
Who tried to use the telephant—
No! No! I mean an elephone
Who tried to use the telephone—
(Dear me! I am not certain quite
That even now I've got it right.)

Howe'er it was, he got his trunk
Entangled in the telephunk;
The more he tried to get it free,
The louder buzzed the telephee—
(I fear I'd better drop the song
Of elephop and telephong!)

Logical English

Anonymous

I said, "This horse, sir, will you shoe?"
　　And soon the horse was shod.
I said, "This deed, sir, will you do?"
　　And soon the deed was dod!

I said, "This stick, sir, will you break?"
　　At once the stick he broke.
I said, "This coat, sir, will you make?"
　　And soon the coat he moke!

Brush Up on Your English

Anonymous

I take it you already know
Of tough and bough and cough and dough
Others may stumble, but not you
On hiccough, thorough, laugh, and through.

And cork and work and card and ward
And font and front and word and sword
Well done! And now if you wish, perhaps
To learn of less familiar traps.

Beware of heard, a dreadful word
That looks like beard and sounds like bird.
And dead: it's said like bed and not like bead—
For goodness sakes don't call it deed.

Watch out for meat and great and threat,
They rhyme with suite and straight and debt.
A moth is not a moth in mothers,
Nor both in bother, broth in brother.

And here is not a match for there,
And dear and fear for bear and pear.
And then there's dose and rose and lose—
Just look them up—and goose and choose,

And do and go, then thwart and cart.
Come, come, I've hardly made a start!
A dreadful language? Man alive!
I'd mastered it when I was five.

Lines and Squares

A. A. Milne

Whenever I walk in a London street,
I'm ever so careful to watch my feet;
    And I keep in the squares,
    And the masses of bears,
Who wait at the corners all ready to eat
The sillies who tread on the lines of the street,
    Go back to their lairs,
    And I say to them, "Bears,
    Just look how I'm walking in all of the squares!"
And the little bears growl to each other, "He's mine,
As soon as he's silly and steps on a line."
And some of the bigger bears try to pretend
That they came round the corner to look for a friend;
And they try to pretend that nobody cares
Whether you walk on the lines or squares.
But only the sillies believe their talk;
It's ever so portant how you walk.
And it's ever so jolly to call out, "Bears,
Just watch me walking in all the squares!"

The Jumblies

Edward Lear

1

They went to sea in a sieve, they did;
   In a sieve they went to sea:
In spite of all their friends could say,
On a winter's morn, on a stormy day,
   In a sieve they went to sea.
And when the sieve turned round and round,
And every one cried, "You'll all be drowned!"
They called aloud, "Our sieve ain't big;
But we don't care a button, we don't care a fig:
   In a sieve we'll go to sea!"
      Far and few, far and few,
         Are the lands where the Jumblies live:
         Their heads are green, and their hands are blue;
         And they went to sea in a sieve.

2

They sailed away in a sieve, they did,
   In a sieve they sailed so fast,
With only a beautiful pea-green veil
Tied with a ribbon, by way of a sail,
   To a small tobacco-pipe mast.
And every one said who saw them go,
"Oh! won't they be soon upset, you know?

For the sky is dark, and the voyage is long;
And, happen what may, it's extremely wrong
   In a sieve to sail so fast."
        Far and few, far and few,
           Are the lands where the Jumblies live:
        Their heads are green, and their hands are blue;
          And they went to sea in a sieve.

3

The water it soon came in, it did;
   The water it soon came in:
So, to keep them dry, they wrapped their feet
In a pinky paper all folded neat;
   And they fastened it down with a pin.
And they passed the night in a crockery-jar;
And each of them said, "How wise we are!
Though the sky be dark, and the voyage be long,
Yet we never can think we were rash or wrong,
   While round in our sieve we spin."
        Far and few, far and few,
           Are the lands where the Jumblies live:
        Their heads are green, and their hands are blue;
          And they went to sea in a sieve.

4

And all night long they sailed away;
   And when the sun went down,
They whistled and warbled a moony song
   To the echoing sound of a coppery gong,
   In the shade of the mountains brown.

"O Timballoo! How happy we are
When we live in a sieve and a crockery-jar!
And all night long, in the moonlight pale,
We sail away with a pea-green sail
  In the shade of the mountains brown."
      Far and few, far and few,
        Are the lands where the Jumblies live:
        Their heads are green, and their hands are blue;
        And they went to sea in a sieve,

5

They sailed to the Western Sea, they did,—
  To a land all covered with trees:
And they bought an owl, and a useful cart,
And a pound of rice, and a cranberry-tart,
  And a hive of silvery bees;
And they bought a pig, and some green jackdaws,
And a lovely monkey with lollipop paws,
And forty bottles of ring-bo-ree,
  And no end of Stilton cheese.
      Far and few, far and few,
        Are the lands where the Jumblies live:
        Their heads are green, and their hands are blue;
        And they went to sea in a sieve.

6

And in twenty years they all came back,—
    In twenty years or more;
And every one said, "How tall they've grown!
For they've been to the Lakes, and the Torrible Zone,
    And the hills of the Chankly Bore."
And they drank their health, and gave them a feast
Of dumplings made of beautiful yeast;
And every one said, "If we only live,
We, too, will go to sea in a sieve,
    To the hills of the Chankly Bore."
        Far and few, far and few,
           Are the lands where the Jumblies live:
           Their heads are green, and their hands are blue;
           And they went to sea in a sieve.

The Pobble Who Has No Toes

Edward Lear

1

The Pobble who has no toes
    Had once as many as we;
When they said, "Some day you may lose them all";
    He replied, "Fish fiddle de-dee!"
And his Aunt Jobiska made him drink
Lavender water tinged with pink;
For she said, "The World in general knows
There's nothing so good for a Pobble's toes!"

2

The Pobble who has no toes,
    Swam across the Bristol Channel;
But before he set out he wrapped his nose
    In a piece of scarlet flannel.
For his Aunt Jobisks said, "No harm
Can come to his toes if his nose is warm;
And it's perfectly known that a Pobble's toes
Are safe—provided he minds his nose."

3

The Pobble swam fast and well.
    And when boats or ships came near him,
He tinkledy-binkledy-winkled a bell
    So that all the world could hear him.

And all the Sailors and Admirals cried,
When they saw him nearing the further side,—
"He has gone to fish, for his Aunt Jobiska's
Runcible Cat with crimson whiskers!"

4

But before he touched the shore,—
    The shore of the Bristol Channel,
A sea-green Porpoise carried away
    His wrapper of scarlet flannel.
And when he came to observe his feet,
Formerly garnished with toes so neat,
His face at once became forlorn
On perceiving that all his toes were gone!

5

And nobody ever knew,
    From that dark day to the present,
Whoso had taken the Pobble's toes,
    In a manner so far from pleasant.
Whether the shrimps or crawfish gray,
Or crafty Mermaids stole them away,
Nobody knew; and nobody knows
How the Pobble was robbed of his twice five toes!

6

The Pobble who has no toes
    Was placed in a friendly Bark,
And they rowed him back, and carried him up
    To his Aunt Jobiska's Park.

And she made him a feast, at his earnest wish,
Of eggs and buttercups fried with fish;
And she said, "It's a fact the whole world knows,
That Pobbles are happier without their toes."

The Owl and the Pussy-Cat

Edward Lear

1

The Owl and the Pussy-Cat went to sea
   In a beautiful pea-green boat:
They took some honey, and plenty of money
   Wrapped up in a five-pound note.
The Owl looked up to the stars above,
   And sang to a small guitar,
"O lovely Pussy, O Pussy, my love,
What a beautiful Pussy you are,
       You are,
       You are!
What a beautiful Pussy you are!"

2

Pussy said to the Owl, "You elegant fowl,
   How charmingly sweet you sing!
Oh! let us be married; too long we have tarried:
   But what shall we do for a ring?"
They sailed away, for a year and a day,
   To the land where the bong-tree grows;
And there in a wood a Piggy-wig stood,
   With a ring at the end of his nose,
       His nose,
       His nose,
   With a ring at the end of his nose.

3

"Dear Pig, are you willing to sell for one shilling
 Your ring?" Said the Piggy, "I will."
So they took it away, and were married next day
 By the Turkey who lives on the hill.
They dined on mince and slices of quince,
 Which they ate with a runcible spoon;
And hand in hand, on the edge of the sand,
 They danced by the light of the moon,
  The moon,
  The moon,
 They danced by the light of the moon.

The Cremation of Sam McGee

Robert Service

There are strange things done in the midnight sun
   By the men who moil for gold;
The Arctic trails have their secret tales
   That would make your blood run cold;
The Northern Lights have seen queer sights,
   But the queerest they ever did see
Was that night on the marge of Lake Lebarge
   I cremated Sam McGee.

Now Sam McGee was from Tennessee, where the cotton
   blooms and blows.
Why he left his home in the South to roam 'round the Pole,
   God only knows.
He was always cold, but the land of gold seemed to hold him
   like a spell;
Though he'd often say in his homely way that "he'd sooner live
   in hell."

On a Christmas Day we were mushing our way over the
   Dawson trail.
Talk of your cold! through the parka's fold it stabbed like a
   driven nail.
If our eyes we'd close, then the lashes froze till sometimes we
   couldn't see;
It wasn't much fun, but the only one to whimper was Sam McGee.

And that very night, as we lay packed tight in our robes
  beneath the snow,
And the dogs were fed, and the stars o'erhead were dancing
  heel and toe,
He turned to me, and "Cap," says he, "I'll cash in this trip,
  I guess;
And if I do, I'm asking that you won't refuse my last request."

Well, he seemed so low that I couldn't say no; then he says
  with a sort of moan:
"It's the cursèd cold, and it's got right hold till I'm chilled
  clean through to the bone.
Yet 'taint being dead—it's my awful dread of the icy grave
  that pains;
So I want you to swear that, foul or fair, you'll cremate my
  last remains."

A pal's last need is a thing to heed, so I swore I would not
  fail;
And we started on at the streak of dawn; but God! he
  looked ghastly pale.
He crouched on the sleigh, and he raved all day of his home
  in Tennessee;
And before nightfall a corpse was all that was left of Sam
  McGee.

There wasn't a breath in that land of death, and I hurried,
  horror-driven,
With a corpse half hid that I couldn't get rid, because of a
  promise given;

It was lashed to the sleigh, and it seemed to say: "You may
  tax your brawn and brains,
But you promised true, and it's up to you to cremate those
  last remains."

Now a promise made is a debt unpaid, and the trail has its
  own stern code.
In the days to come, though my lips were dumb, in my heart
  how I cursed that load.
In the long, long night, by the lone firelight, while the
  huskies, round in a ring,
Howled out their woes to the homeless snows—O God!
  how I loathed the thing.

And every day that quiet clay seemed to heavy and heavier
  grow;
And on I went, though the dogs were spent and the grub
  was getting low;
The trail was bad, and I felt half mad, but I swore I would
  not give in;
And I'd often sing to the hateful thing, and it hearkened
  with a grin.

Till I came to the marge of Lake Lebarge, and a derelict
  there lay;
It was jammed in the ice, but I saw in a trice it was called the
  "Alice May."
And I looked at it, and I thought a bit, and I looked at my
  frozen chum;
Then "Here," said I, with a sudden cry, "is my cre-ma-tor-eum."

Some planks I tore from the cabin floor, and I lit the boiler
  fire;
Some coal I found that was lying around, and I heaped the
  fuel higher;
The flames just soared, and the furnace roared—such a
  blaze you seldom see;
And I burrowed a hole in the glowing coal, and I stuffed in
  Sam McGee.

Then I made a hike, for I didn't like to hear him sizzle so;
And the heavens scowled, and the huskies howled, and the
  wind began to blow.
It was icy cold, but the hot sweat rolled down my cheeks,
  and I don't know why;
And the greasy smoke in an inky cloak went streaking
  down the sky.

I do not know how long in the snow I wrestled with grisly
  fear;
But the stars came out and they danced about ere again I
  ventured near;
I was sick with dread, but I bravely said: "I'll just take a
  peep inside.
I guess he's cooked, and it's time I looked";...then the door
  I opened wide.

And there sat Sam, looking cool and calm, in the heart of
  the furnace roar;
And he wore a smile you could see a mile, and he said:
  "Please close that door.

It's fine in here, but I greatly fear you'll let in the cold and
    storm—
Since I left Plumtree, down in Tennessee, it's the first time
    I've been warm."

    There are strange things done in the midnight sun
        By the men who moil for gold;
    The Arctic trails have their secret tales
        That would make your blood run cold;
    The Northern Lights have seen queer sights,
        But the queerest they ever did see
    Was that night on the marge of Lake Lebarge
        I cremated Sam McGee.

Casey at the Bat

Ernest Lawrence Thayer

The outlook wasn't brilliant for the Mudville nine that day;
The score stood four to two with but one inning more to
play.
And then when Cooney died at first and Barrows did the
same,
A sickly silence fell upon the patrons of the game.

A straggling few got up to go in deep despair. The rest
Clung to the hope which springs eternal in the human
breast;
They thought if only Casey could but get a whack at that—
We'd put up even money now with Casey at the bat.

But Flynn preceded Casey, as did also Jimmy Blake,
And the former was a lulu and the latter was a cake;
So upon that stricken multitude grim melancholy sat,
For there seemed but little chance of Casey's getting to
the bat.

But Flynn let drive a single, to the wonderment of all,
And Blake, the much despisèd, tore the cover off the ball;
And when the dust had lifted, and the men saw what had
occurred,
There was Jimmy safe at second and Flynn a-hugging third.

Then from five thousand throats and more there rose a
   lusty yell;
It rumbled through the valley, it rattled in the dell;
It knocked upon the mountain and recoiled upon the flat,
For Casey, mighty Casey, was advancing to the bat.

There was ease in Casey's manner as he stepped into his
   place;
There was pride in Casey's bearing and a smile on Casey's
   face.
And when, responding to the cheers, he lightly doffed his
   hat,
No stranger in the crowd could doubt 'twas Casey at the
   bat.

Ten thousand eyes were on him as he rubbed his hands
   with dirt;
Five thousand tongues applauded when he wiped them on
   his shirt.
Then while the writhing pitcher ground the ball into his hip,
Defiance gleamed in Casey's eye, a sneer curled Casey's lip.

And now the leather-covered sphere came hurtling
   through the air,
And Casey stood a-watching it in haughty grandeur there.
Close by the sturdy batsman the ball unheeded sped—
"That ain't my style," said Casey. "Strike one," the umpire
   said.

From the benches, black with people, there went up a
    muffled roar,
Like the beating of the storm waves on a stern and distant
    shore.
"Kill him! Kill the umpire!" shouted someone on the
    stand;
And it's likely they'd have killed him had not Casey raised
    his hand.

With a smile of Christian charity great Casey's visage
    shone;
He stilled the rising tumult; he bade the game go on;
He signaled to the pitcher, and once more the spheroid
    flew;
But Casey still ignored it, and the umpire said, "Strike two."

"Fraud!" cried the maddened thousands, and echo
    answered, "Fraud!"
But one scornful look from Casey and the audience was
    awed.
They saw his face grow stern and cold, they saw his muscles
    strain,
And they knew that Casey wouldn't let that ball go by
    again.

The sneer is gone from Casey's lip, his teeth are clenched in
    hate;
He pounds with cruel violence his bat upon the plate.
And now the pitcher holds the ball, and now he lets it go,
And now the air is shattered by the force of Casey's blow.

Oh, somewhere in this favored land the sun is shining
    bright;
The band is playing somewhere, and somewhere hearts are
    light,
And somewhere men are laughing, and somewhere
    children shout;
But there is no joy in Mudville—mighty Casey has struck
    out.

The Purple Cow

Gelett Burgess

I never saw a Purple Cow,
   I never hope to see one,
But I can tell you, anyhow,
   I'd rather see than be one!

Table Manners

Gelett Burgess

The Goops they lick their fingers,
    And the Goops they lick their knives;
They spill their broth on the tablecloth—
    Oh, they lead disgusting lives!
The Goops they talk while eating,
    And loud and fast they chew;
And that is why I'm glad that I
    Am not a Goop—are you?

As I Was Walking up the Stair

Hughes Mearns

As I was walking up the stair
I met a man who wasn't there;
He wasn't there again today.
I wish, I wish he'd stay away.

As I Was Going to St. Ives

Anonymous

As I was going to St. Ives,
I met a man with seven wives.
Every wife had seven sacks,
Every sack had seven cats,
Every cat had seven kits.
Kits, cats, sacks, and wives,
How many were going to St. Ives?

Solomon Grundy

Anonymous

Solomon Grundy,
Born on Monday,
Christened on Tuesday,
Married on Wednesday,
Took ill on Thursday,
Worse on Friday,
Died on Saturday,
Buried on Sunday;
This is the end
Of Solomon Grundy!

Daddy Fell into the Pond

Alfred Noyes

Everyone grumbled. The sky was gray.
We had nothing to do and nothing to say.
We were nearing the end of a dismal day,
And there seemed to be nothing beyond,
   THEN
     Daddy fell into the pond!

And everyone's face grew merry and bright,
And Timothy danced for sheer delight.
"Give me the camera, quick, oh quick!
He's crawling out of the duckweed." *Click!*

Then the gardener suddenly slapped his knee.
And doubled up, shaking silently,
And the ducks all quacked as if they were daft,
And it sounded as if the old drake laughed.
Oh, there wasn't a thing that didn't respond
   WHEN
     Daddy fell into the pond!

I Wandered Lonely as a Clod

The Editors of *MAD* Magazine

I wandered lonely as a clod,
Just picking up old rags and bottles,
When onward on my way I plod,
I saw a host of axolotls;
Beside the lake, beneath the trees,
A sight to make a man's blood freeze.

Some had handles, some were plain;
They came in blue, red, pink, and green.
A few were orange in the main;
The damndest sight I've ever seen.
The females gave a sprightly glance;
The male ones all wore knee-length pants.

Now oft, when on the couch I lie,
The doctor asks me what I see.
They flash upon my inward eye
And make me laugh in fiendish glee.
I find my solace then in bottles,
And I forget them axolotls.

A Boy Named Sue

Shel Silverstein

Well, daddy left home when I was three
And he didn't leave much to ma and me,
Just this old guitar and an empty bottle of booze
Now, I don't blame him because he run and hid
But the meanest thing that he ever did
Was before he left, he went and named me Sue

Well, he must have thought it was quite a joke,
And it got a lots of laughs from lots of folk,
It seems I had to fight my whole life through.
Some gal would giggle and I'd get red,
And some guy would laugh and I'd bust his head and
I tell you life ain't easy for a boy named Sue.

Well, I grew up quick and I grew up mean,
My fist got hard and my wits got keen.
Roamed from town to town to hide my shame,
But I made me a vow to the moon and stars,
I'd search the honky-tonks and bars
And kill that man that give me that awful Name.

But it was Gatlinburg in mid-July
And I just hit town and my throat was dry.
I'd thought I'd stop and have myself a brew.
At an old saloon on a street of mud
And at a table dealing stud
Sat the dirty, mangy dog that named me Sue.

Well I knew that snake was my own sweet dad
From a worn-out picture that my mother had.
And I know that scar on his cheek and his evil eye.
He was big and bent and gray and old
And I looked at him and my blood ran cold,
And I said, "My name is Sue, how do you do.
Now you're gonna die."

Well I hit him right between the eyes
And he went down, but to my surprise
He come up with a knife and cut off a piece of my ear.
But I busted a chair right across his teeth.
And we crashed through the wall and into the street
Kicking and a-gouging in the mud and the blood and the
    beer.

I tell you I've fought tougher men
But I really can't remember when.
He kicked like a mule and he bit like a crocodile.
I heard him laughin' and then I heard him cussin',
He went for his gun and I pulled mine first.
He stood there looking at me and I saw him smile.

And he said, "Son, this world is rough
And if a man's gonna make it, he's gotta be tough
And I know I wouldn't be there to help you along.
So I give you that name and I said goodbye.
I knew you'd have to get tough or die.
And it's the name that helped to make you strong."

Yeah, he said "now you have just fought one helluva
    fight,
And I know you hate me and you've got the right
To kill me now and I wouldn't blame you if you do.
But you ought to thank me before I die
For the gravel in your guts and the spit in your eye
Because I'm the . . . That named you Sue."

I got all choked up and I threw down my gun.
Called him my pa, and he called me a son,
And I come away with a different point of view,
And I think about him now and then.
Every time I tried, every time I win
And if I ever have a son I think I'm gonna name him
Bill or George—anything but Sue!

Falling Up

Shel Silverstein

I tripped on my shoelace
And I fell up—
Up to the roof tops,
Up over the town,
Up past the tree tops,
Up over the mountains,
Up where the colors
Blend into the sounds.
But it got me so dizzy
When I looked around,
I got sick to my stomach
And I threw down.

Boa Constrictor

Shel Silverstein

I'm being eaten
By a Boa Constrictor,
A Boa Constrictor,
A Boa Constrictor,
I'm being eaten by a Boa Constrictor,
And I don't like it one bit.
Whadaya know?
It's nibblin' my toe.
Oh, gee,
It's up to my knee.
Oh fiddle,
It's up to my middle
Oh, heck,
It's up to my neck;
Oh, dread
It's mmmmmmmmmmfffffffff

Ladybird, Ladybird

Anonymous

Ladybird, ladybird,
　Fly away home,
Your house is on fire
　And your children all gone;

All except one
　And that's little Ann
And she has crept under
　The warming pan.

There Was a Crooked Man

Anonymous

There was a crooked man, and he walked a crooked mile,
He found a crooked sixpence against a crooked stile;
He bought a crooked cat, which caught a crooked mouse,
And they all lived together in a little crooked house.

It's Raining, It's Pouring

Anonymous

It's raining, it's pouring,
The old man's snoring;
He got into bed
And bumped his head
And couldn't get up in the morning.

Don't Worry If Your Job Is Small

Anonymous

Don't worry if your job is small,
And your rewards are few.
Remember that the mighty oak,
Was once a nut like you.

Acknowledgments

"Boa Constrictor." Words and Music by Shel Silverstein. TRO © Copyright 1962 (Renewed) 1968 (Renewed) 1969 (Renewed) Hollis Music, Inc., New York, NY. Used by permission.

"A Boy Named Sue." Words and Music by Shel Silverstein. © Copyright 1969 (Renewed) Evil Eye Music, Inc. West Palm Beach, FL. Used by permission.

"The Boy Who Laughed at Santa Claus" by Ogden Nash. Copyright © 1936 by Odgen Nash. Reprinted by permission of Curtis Brown, Ltd.

"Daddy Fell into the Pond" by Alfred Noyes. 1952. Reprinted by permission of The Society of Authors

"Eletelephony" from TIRRA LIRRA by Laura Richards. Copyright © 1930, 1932 by Laura E. Richards; Copyright © renewed 1960 by Hamilton Richards. By permission of Little, Brown and Company.

"Falling Up" by Shel Silverstein. Copyright © 1996. Evil Eye Music, Inc. Used by permission of HarperCollins Publishers.

"I Wandered Lonely as a Clod." © 1958 E.C. Publications, Inc. All Rights Reserved. Used with Permission.

"Lines and Squares" from WHEN WE WERE VERY YOUNG by A. A. Milne, illustrations by E. H. Shepard, copyright 1924 by E. P. Dutton, renewed 1952 by A. A. Milne. Used by permission of Dutton Children's Books, A Division of Penguin Young Readers Group, A Member of Penguin Group (USA) Inc., 345 Hudson Street, New York, NY 10014. All rights reserved.

Index to Titles
and Authors